The Cheese Buyer's Handbook

The Cheese Buyer's Handbook

Daniel O'Keefe

Photographer: Reg Morrison

McGraw-Hill Book Company

New York   St. Louis   San Francisco
Toronto   Dusseldorf   Mexico

ACKNOWLEDGEMENTS

The following organisations and companies provided information and assistance in the compilation of this book: the Australian Dairy Corporation; the Danish Cheese Export Board; the English Country Cheese Council; Norwegian Dairies; the Dutch Dairy Bureau; the German Dairy Board; Alta Lipids Australia Pty Ltd; the photograph of Brick cheese was supplied by the American Dairy Association; the photograph of Liederkranz cheese was provided by Borden Foods, Ohio; the illustrations of stages in the cheesemaking process were provided by the Australian Dairy Board. Works consulted during the research were Androuet's *Guide du Fromage*, Marquis and Haskell's *The Cheese Book*, the US Department of Agriculture's publication *Cheeses of the World* and Simon's *Cheeses of the World*.

Special thanks to Mr David Golante of The Cheese Board, Manhattan, New York, for his advice on American cheeses and also to Maureen and Ian Nathan of the International Cheese Shop, Crows Nest, Sydney, for general consultation on the book.

Library of Congress Cataloging in Publication Data

O'Keefe, Daniel
    The Cheese buyer's handbook.
    1. Cheese.   I. Title.
TX382.O33   641.3'7'3   78-8530
ISBN 0-07-047660-8

Published in the United States by
McGraw-Hill Book Company, 1978

This book was designed and produced by
Paul Hamlyn Pty Limited, Australia

Printed in Hong Kong

CONTENTS

THE WORLD OF CHEESE

Cheese is one of the most varied and subtle foods in the world. In taste cheese can be bland, buttery, innocuous, rich, creamy, pungent, sharp, salty or lightly delicate. In texture it can be hard enough to chip off in flakes, so soft and runny that it needs to be eaten with a spoon—or at any one of a dozen points of softness and firmness between these two extremes. In aroma, cheese can be rank and overpowering enough to turn the stomach of the strongest man (and still be eaten with relish by devotees), delicately aromatic or virtually unnoticeable. Cheese can serve as the perfect companion for wines, a superbly satisfying finale to a gourmet meal or simply as a basic nourishing foodstuff for family snacks.

It is this variety of character that has made cheese so appreciated as a food for hundreds, even thousands, of years. The reason for this is that the cheesemaking process, while following the same broad pattern, is subjected to numerous variations in types of milk, cheesemaking techniques and the length of the time given to maturing. The differences in textures, flavours and aromas of different cheeses are the result of these numerous variations.

Thus cheeses offer an enormous range—from the rich delicacy of a Brie or a Camembert to the full 'bite' of a mature Cheddar and the sharp piercing saltiness of a Feta. And while every cheese is not to every taste, it is fair to say that almost everyone can find a cheese to suit his or her taste.

Cheese is also one of the most nutritious of foods. A cheese with a fat content of 48 per cent has a protein content in the region of 23-25 per cent, making the protein value of 210 g (7 oz) of such a cheese equal to 300 g (10 oz) of meat. In one solid, compact form, cheese also contains calcium, phosphorus, mineral salts and varying amounts of A and B and other vitamins.

Of course most cheeses are also high in calories, a fact that causes many people concerned with their weight to be wary.

A cheese's calorie count can be judged from the fat content which most cheeses have detailed on their packaging. The fat content refers to the percentage of butterfat in the dry matter of the cheese. The Dutch, for example, class their cheeses as:

- full-cream cheese—48 per cent fat content
- 40+ —at least 40 per cent fat content
- 20+ —at least 20 per cent fat content
- 4+ (skim milk cheese)—4 per cent fat content

While it is true that many cheeses do have a high calorie count, this does not apply to them all. Cottage Cheese, depending on whether it is creamed or not, has a butterfat content varying between 4 and 15 per cent; the German sour curd cheeses such as Harz and Mainz have a fat content under 10 per cent, and Australia has recently developed a fat modified Cheddar-style cheese marketed as Altapol.

It is worth remembering, too, the overall composition of cheese when considering its fat content. The softer the cheese the higher its moisture content will be. Thus soft cheeses such as Camembert and Brie can contain up to 50 per cent water—therefore their fat content (45-50 per cent) need only be counted against half of what you eat. On the other hand, the fat content of Emmentaler (45 per cent) cannot be considered so reducible as Emmentaler is a hard cheese which has had a large degree of moisture drained from it.

At the top end of the fat-content scale lie the double and triple crème cheeses, which can have a fat content of from 60 to 75 per cent. If you develop a passion for these, it is probably best that you take up jogging.

THE HISTORY OF CHEESE

Most authorities consider that cheese was first made in the Middle East. The earliest type was a form of sour milk which came into being when it was discovered that domesticated animals could be milked. A legendary story has it that cheese was 'discovered' by an unknown Arab nomad. He is said to have filled a saddlebag with milk to sustain him on a journey across the desert by horse. After several hours riding he stopped to quench his thirst, only to find that the milk had separated into a pale watery liquid and solid white lumps. Because the saddlebag, which was made from the stomach of a young animal, contained a coagulating enzyme known as rennin, the milk had been effectively separated into curds and whey by the combination of the rennin, the hot sun and the galloping motions of the horse. The nomad, unconcerned with technical details, found the whey drinkable and the curds edible.

Cheese was known to the ancient Sumerians four thousand years before the birth of Christ. The ancient Greeks credited Aristaeus, a son of Apollo and Cyrene, with its discovery; it is mentioned in the Old Testament.

In the Roman era cheese really came into its own. Cheesemaking was done with skill and knowledge and reached a high standard. By this time the ripening process had been developed and it was known that various treatments and conditions under storage resulted in different flavours and characteristics.

The larger Roman houses had a separate cheese kitchen, the *caseale*, and also special areas where cheese could be matured. In large towns home-made cheese could be taken to a special centre to be smoked. Cheese was served on the tables of the nobility and travelled to the far corners of the Roman Empire as a regular part of the rations of the legions.

During the Middle Ages, monks became innovators and developers and it is to them we owe many of the classic varieties of cheese marketed today. During the Renaissance period cheese suffered a drop in popularity, being considered unhealthy, but it regained favour by the nineteenth century, the period that saw the start of the move from farm to factory production.

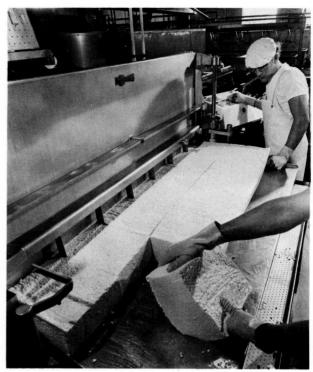

Cutting the cheese curd before 'cheddaring'.

CHEESEMAKING

Cheese is made from milk; in the main it is made from cow's milk but there are many varieties made from sheep's milk and goat's milk. Cheese is also made from the milk of buffaloes (Mozzarella is one), reindeer, asses, camels and most domesticated herbivores (let it be added, however, that it is unlikely that your local cheese supplier is going to be pressing huge stocks of reindeer's, asses' or camel's milk cheese upon you).

The basic principle involved in making all natural cheese is to coagulate or curdle the milk so that it forms into curds (milky white lumps) and whey (a thin liquid). As anyone knows who has left milk unrefrigerated for a period, milk will curdle quite naturally. The milk sours and forms into an acid curd. This is the basis of nearly all cheesemaking (whey cheeses are the exception, being made from the whey of the milk rather than the curds). Today's methods help the curdling process by the addition of a *starter* (a bacterial culture which produces lactic acid) and *rennet* (a

The beginning of the 'cheddaring' process. The drained cheese curd is turned and stacked at the bottom of the cheese vat at intervals of ten to fifteen minutes for about one-and-a-half hours.

Salting—here the cheese is being immersed in a brine bath. Salting plays an important role in rind formation.

Milling Cheddar cheese. The cheese is milled into small curd pieces, salted, then placed in cloth-lined metal hoops.

Storing and maturing blue vein cheese. Note the inoculation needles in the foreground. These needles allow air to penetrate into the body of the cheese to promote the growth of the veining.

substance obtained from the stomach linings of young calves which contains a coagulating enzyme which speeds the separation of liquids and solids).

The least sophisticated cheeses are the fresh, unripened varieties typified by Cottage Cheese. These are made by warming the milk and letting it stand, treating it with a lactic starter to help the acid development and then cutting and draining the whey from the cheese. The cheese is then packed and marketed without further ripening. This is the simplest, most basic form of cheese.

Cheeses that undergo a ripening process (also known as a curing, maturing or ageing process) are all treated with rennet. Before the ripening process begins, they go through a sequence of operations which, while following the same general pattern, varies from cheese to cheese. Basically, this sequence is:

- milk is warmed
- a starter culture and rennet are added
- the milk coagulates into a single huge curd
- the curd is stirred and cut to drain off whey
- the curd is heated, sometimes pressed, to remove more whey
- the curd is moulded and shaped into a cheese, salting taking place before or after this process
- the cheese is matured under controlled conditions.

Variations on the cheesemaking process start with the milk. It may be taken from a morning or an evening milking, or from a combination of both. Before the milk is set a colouring agent may be added to it, the most widely used one being annatto, a vegetable dye taken from a South American plant. This produces an amber-orange-yellow colour. The milk may be skimmed of its cream content or have cream added to it. The quality of the milk, its richness, its acid content, the degree to which it is heated, even the breed of cow that is used, the grass she feeds on, the soil and the climate—all these factors influence the final cheese.

So does the amount of rennet used, the way the cheese is pressed, the heating of the curds, the degree of salting, the number of times the cheese is turned from one side to another while it is maturing, how the cheese is brushed, scraped or washed and the ingredients used to treat the cheese (Appenzell is immersed for a period in a mixture of white wine and spices, Maroilles is bathed with beer, Feta matures in brine and so forth.)

During the ripening period, the two most important factors are the length of the maturing time (it can vary from two weeks to seven years) and the temperature at which the cheese is matured.

It is during this time that the micro-organisms play their part. They may be present naturally in the milk or in the atmosphere of the curing room, or they can be artificially introduced.

Blue veined cheeses are inoculated with a *Penicillium* spore which creates their aroma, flavour and bluish or greenish veining. Such cheeses are internally moulded and ripen from the inside out. On the other hand, cheeses such as Camembert and Brie have their surfaces treated with a different type of *Penicillium* spore which creates a downy white mould (known as a bloomy or flowery rind): this makes them surface ripened cheeses.

Many surface ripened cheeses have their surfaces smeared with a bacterial broth. With others the bacteria is in the atmosphere of the curing chambers. These cheeses are called washed rind varieties as they must be washed regularly during their ripening period (longer than for Camembert or Brie) to prevent their interiors drying out. The washings also help promote an even bacterial growth across the surfaces of the cheeses. As this washing can be done with liquids as diverse as salt water and brandy, it also plays a part in the final flavour of the cheese.

The rinds of the cheeses are formed during the ripening process, many quite naturally. Some, as we have seen, artificially. Rinds may be brushed, washed, oiled, treated with a covering of paraffin wax or simply not touched at all. Traditional Cheddars are wrapped around with a cotton bandage. The rind's basic function is to protect the interior of the cheese and allow it to ripen harmoniously. Its presence thus affects the final flavour of the cheese. Salting plays an important role in rind formation. Heavily salted cheeses develop a thick, tough outer rind, typified by the Swiss range of cheeses. Cheddar, another natural-rind cheese, is less salted than the Swiss varieties, and consequently has a much thinner rind.

A batch of Australian Gouda cheese maturing.

Mention too needs to be made of pasteurisation. On the Continent, many cheeses are made from raw, unpasteurised milk. Outside Europe, however, most cheeses are made from pasteurised milk. American federal laws, for example state that all unripened cheese must be made from pasteurised milk and so also must all ripened cheeses, unless they are aged for a period of at least sixty days. Similarly, all English and Australian cheese is made from pasteurised milk. While the interests of hygiene may be best served in this way, cheeses made from pasteurised milk never develop the full character and personality of cheeses made from unpasteurised milk, simply because many of the micro-organisms responsible have been effectively destroyed.

Processed cheese, as opposed to natural cheese, takes this one stage further. Here the actual cheese (usually a combination of two cheeses), rather than the milk, is subjected to a heat treatment at a given point. Because of this the cheese does not continue to mature and develop in flavour, but remains constant in taste throughout its life.

CHEESE TYPES

Cheese can be placed into various family groups or types. The groupings are, however, somewhat arbitrary and vary from authority to authority. The Australian Dairy Board, for example, classes all cheeses made in Australia as fresh, soft, firm or hard. The Board classes as fresh cheeses Cottage, Cream, and Ricotta; as firm cheeses Cheddar, Cheshire, Edam, Gouda, Provolone, Taffel, Samsoe and Swiss (Emmentaler); and as hard cheeses Parmesan, Pecorino, Pepato and Romano.

The US Department of Agriculture classes cheeses as very hard, hard, semi-soft or soft. It considers Cheddar a hard cheese rather than firm and blue veins as semi-soft rather than soft. The Department, in a publication first produced in 1953, also states that there are about eighteen types of natural cheeses, listing them as Brick, Camembert, Cheddar, Cottage, Cream, Edam, Gouda, Hand, Limburger, Neufchâtel, Parmesan, Provolone, Romano, Roquefort, Sapsago, Swiss, Trappist and whey

cheese. The Department adds, however, that such a grouping, while informative, is 'imperfect and incomplete'.

The French cheese expert Pierre Androuet, in his book *Guide de Fromage*, an excellent and detailed study principally of French cheeses, is more exact. Apart from fresh cheeses and processed cheeses he classifies cheeses into six family groups by their nature and type of rind. They are: bloomy-rind cheeses such as Camembert and Brie; wash-rind cheeses such as Limburger, Maroilles and Livarot; natural-rind goat's milk cheeses; blue veins; semi-soft uncooked pressed cheeses such as Saint Paulin; and hard or cooked cheeses such as Parmesan and Emmentaler.

For the layman, probably the easiest way to identify cheese types is to place the cheese in groupings based on how they are made and similarities of appearance and flavour. The classification used in this book attempts this. It should be said that although not all cheeses within a grouping will taste alike, they should be more similar in taste than cheeses placed in other groups. It will also be seen that some cheeses can be placed in more than one group.

Fresh, unripened cheeses: These are cheeses which do not undergo a maturing process and include Cottage, Cream and Ricotta. In taste they are the mildest, least flavoursome of all cheeses. They are usually not salted.

Double and Triple crèmes: These cheeses have been heavily enriched with cream during their manufacturing process. The double crèmes have a fat content of 60 per cent, and the triple crèmes a 75 per cent fat content. This makes them all exceptionally rich, creamy and luscious. Some of them do not undergo a ripening process, so they can also be classed as unripened cheeses. Petit Suisse is a case in point. Although it is not ripened, its fat content can vary between 60 and 75 per cent. Other double and triple crèmes are cured for about three weeks before marketing and develop a very thin, downy rind. These include Boursault, Brillat-Savarin and Excelsior. Others such as Blue Castello and Bavarian Blue have a blue veining. While double and triple crèmes can vary in flavour and style, they have in common a degree of richness and creaminess not present in other cheeses.

Bland and buttery: Into this category can be placed a great variety of essentially mild tasting, stable, all-purpose table cheeses. These cheeses are unpronounced in flavour and aroma—which is not to say that they are without distinction. The range is considerable and includes the Samsoe group, Edam, Gouda, Bel Paese and Fontina. Such cheeses are usually firm and supple-textured, easily sliceable and make excellent lunch, breakfast or sandwich snacks. Many are of sufficient quality to be served at end of meals.

Swiss-style cheeses: The most famous of these is Emmentaler with its tough outer rind, distinctive holes or 'eyes' and characteristic mild, sweetish, nutty flavour. Relatives of Emmentaler include Appenzell, Gruyère, Royalp, Sbrinz and Raclette. Swiss-style cheeses usually have tough hard rinds and interiors dotted with holes. These holes are caused by expansion of gas within the cheese curd during the ripening period.

Cheddar-style cheeses: Cheddar is one of the most popular and widely copied cheeses in the world. Cheeses that are 'cheddared' undergo a step in the making process which involves them being cut into pieces and stacked and turned at the bottom of the cheese vat for a period. The archetypal Cheddar cheese is firm-textured, yellow in colour with a clean, mellow taste which develops a sharp and tangy bite the further it matures. English cheeses such as Gloucester, Cheshire, Leicester, Lancashire, Derby, Wensleydale and Caerphilly all belong to the Cheddar family. Even Stilton, a blue vein, is Cheddar based. America, Australia, Canada and New Zealand all make varieties of Cheddar in varying degrees of strength. Vermont is one of the best-known American types and the Canadian Cheddars, made from unpasteurised milk, are highly rated. Cantal is a French Cheddar-style cheese and Kashkaval is a distant Greek relative made from sheep's milk.

Extra-hard cheeses: The majority of these cheeses are the Italian Grana style. They have an exceptionally hard, brittle texture which makes them suitable for grating and are known for their exquisitely sharp, piquant flavour.

Cheeses of this type can be matured for up to three years. Parmesan is the best known of the group but the Swiss Sbrinz and Sapsago cheeses also fit into the category. Saanen, also Swiss, is sometimes matured for seven years. Young versions of some grating cheeses are used as table cheeses.

Monastery cheeses: Cheeses in this group are often linked historically in that they have monastic origins. Such cheeses as Port Salut, Saint Paulin, the various forms of Trappist cheese made throughout the world, Esrom and Harvarti have similarities of taste, although varying degrees of strength of flavour and aroma. Several mountain cheeses, such as Beaumont and Reblochon, are also classified as monastery type cheeses. The majority of monastery cheeses are of the washed rind variety.

Blue veins: These cheeses are characterised by their internal veining of blue, blue-black or green, and their pungent aromas and tangy flavours. All blue-vein cheeses are internally ripened after being inoculated with a *Penicillium* spore. They are usually classed as soft cheeses but can be crumbly in texture. Some, however, are exceptionally soft, even to the point of spreadability. Roquefort, Stilton and Gorgonzola are considered the three best blue veins in the world.

Camembert and Brie types: These cheeses are known as bloomy or flowery-rind cheeses because of the light, downy white rind that grows on their surfaces, the result of their being treated with the *Penicillium candidum* spore. The interior paste of this sort of cheese is soft and straw yellow in colour. If the cheese is at its peak, the paste bulges out from beneath the rind when the cheese is cut. Tangy, richly delicate and delicious in flavour, Camembert and Brie are widely copied, but the French versions, of which there are many, are generally acknowledged as the best and the most full-flavoured. Other cheeses of this type include Carré de l'Est, Coulommiers and Chaource.

Goat's milk cheeses: Distinctively different in taste to cow's milk cheeses, these cheeses come in a variety of shapes and sizes such as pyramids, cones and cylinders, all usually quite

small. All have a characteristic barnyard or 'goaty' quality to their flavour, but whether this is mild or pronounced depends on how long the cheese has been aged. Some are quite delicate; others are ferociously pungent and rank. All French goat's milk cheeses are called *chèvres*—and today many are made from a mixture of goat's milk and cow's or sheep's milk.

Sheep's milk cheeses: Like goat's milk cheeses, these cheeses taste quite different to cow's milk varieties. Their flavour ranges from mild to sharp. Some are noticeably salty, the result of being matured in brine. Many of the traditional Greek cheeses fall into this category, Feta being best known. Others, like Kashkaval and Kasseri, have a noticeable 'sheepy' flavour —a sourish tang, distinctive and attractive and, like many goat's milk cheeses, vaguely 'barn-yardy'.

Spiced or flavoured cheeses: Many cheeses have their flavours enhanced by the addition of a variety of herbs and spices. Derby Sage has a greenish hue due to sage being introduced to the cheese curd during the making process (Vermont Sage is the American equivalent); Leyden is treated with caraway and cumin seeds; and Boursin, a triple-crème cheese, is marketed in flavoured versions ranging from pepper to garlic. Other cheeses may be studded with walnuts, covered with grape seeds or treated with cloves. The English are now producing several of their traditional lines flavoured with beer, wine, cider, port and chives.

Smoked cheeses: Smoked cheese is simply a cheese variety, often Cheddar or Emmentaler, which has been treated and flavoured with smoke. Most of this type of cheese is processed. It is often made in traditional sausage shapes. In most cases the smoke flavour is produced by chemicals rather than by hanging the cheeses over a fire. Smoked cheeses are often additionally flavoured with ingredients ranging from caraway seeds to a textured vegetable protein tasting like ham.

Whey cheeses: While the great majority of cheeses are made from the curds of the milk, there are some which are made from the whey. Gjetöst, a cheese totally distinctive in looks and taste, is one. It has milk sugar (lactose) and cream added to it during the making process and looks like a chunk of chocolate fudge. Ricotta, already classed as an unripened cheese, is also made from whey but is basically an Italian version of Cottage Cheese. It has nothing in common, in either taste or appearance, with Gjetöst—except that it is a whey cheese.

Strong-smelling cheeses: Probably the best known cheese in this category is Limburger, Belgian in origin but often thought of as German due to its great popularity in that country. Cheeses that possess a truly powerful aroma are usually of the washed rind variety. For many people the aroma is both the beginning and the end of the acquaintance. A legendary story about Limburger recounts the uproar that was created in a small town in Green County, Wisconsin, when a cartload of ripened Limburgers was left unattended in a main street. The fact is that cheeses such as Limburger, Maroilles and Livarot are extremely pungent smelling, not to say rank, and overpowering. In Limburger's case, its bark is somewhat less than its bite, for the cheese's taste is not as strong as its smell. Maroilles and Livarot, however, are both strong-smelling and strong-tasting, as are the German matured varieties of sour curd cheeses such as Harz and Mainz (the American version of this style of cheese is known as Hand). Brick and Liederkranz, the two cheeses that are considered genuine American originals, are also noted for their distinctive aromas, but unless well aged they are not overpronounced in taste.

Processed cheese: All processed cheese has its ripening process arrested at a given point by heat treatment. It is usually made from one or two cheese types blended together and can never develop the individuality of flavour of natural cheese because the micro-organisms that create such things are effectively killed off. For many people processed cheeses taste 'plastic' and innocuous but nevertheless they are enormously popular—partly because of their keeping properties, their economy and their blandness. Today there is an enormous range of processed cheese on the market, flavoured by a staggering variety of ingredients which range from salmon to pineapple.

A selection of Provolone and Mozzarella cheeses (photo by Russell Cockayne)

KEEPING AND STORING

It was tempting to discuss the maximum time that a cheese will keep, but as most people will buy cheese by the piece, there seemed little point in doing this. Once a cheese has been cut it loses the protection of its rind and starts to deteriorate.

If you buy a whole cheese and store it correctly it is quite possible it will keep for more than a year, if not cut. Storing whole, uncut cheeses, however, is an involved business. Besides needing the right conditions—a cool, moist, well ventilated room, free of draughts—cheeses need a certain amount of attention. Remember too, that cheese, like wine, is a living substance that will continue to develop the longer it is stored, and you may end up with a cheese whose flavour is quite different from the one you originally envisaged.

The amount of time any cheese will keep is dependent on its moisture content. Fresh cheeses with a high moisture content need to be eaten within a short time after purchase, while extra-hard grating cheese will keep almost indefinitely. Correctly stored, a firm-textured cheese like Cheddar, when cut, will keep for several weeks, as will a semi-soft cheese like Saint Paulin. Bloomy rind cheese such as Brie and Camembert have a limited life when cut and should be eaten as soon as possible.

Probably the best course for the average cheese buyer is to buy in small quantities—that is, buy only what you are capable of eating within one to two weeks. A major exception are the hard grating cheeses such as Parmesan. A cut piece of Parmesan cheese, provided it is well wrapped and stored, will keep for a considerable length of time.

Cut cheese should be kept in a refrigerator, wrapped in airtight aluminium foil, plastic film or bags. If you are storing several types of cheese, they should of course be wrapped individually. Before serving, the cheese should be removed from the refrigerator for at least two hours so that it is given sufficient time to reach room temperature before consumption, otherwise you will not get the benefit of its true flavour. Cheese for immediate consumption can be kept under a cheese dome. It is a useful trick to place under the edge of the dome a small object such as a piece of sugar to allow the water vapour given off by the cheese to escape. Do not store cheese under a dome. Cheese can be frozen, but this is not really recommended. Texture and flavour are likely to be affected—and for the worse.

Should a mould spot develop on a cheese, simply cut it off. The rest of the cheese will not be adversely affected, unless the mould is widespread.

CHEESE AND WINE

Cheese and wine are a natural combination but they will not join forces indiscriminately. A cheese with a full aroma and strong flavour will not go well with a delicate wine that has a subtle bouquet—the cheese will overwhelm the wine. A practical rule of thumb is—the more body the wine has, the more full-flavoured the cheese may be. So do not serve a soft-flavoured little-accented cheese with a heavy wine. Similarly, do not serve a light and elegant wine with a sharp and tangy cheese.

In this book only the general characteristics of the wine style most suited to the particular cheese are described. Although there is a world trend towards describing wines by the grape variety from which they are made and the regional characteristics of the area in which the grapes are grown, this trend is not yet universally established. The wines in this book have consequently been described in general terms as sweet or dry, red or white, fruity, full-bodied, aged, et cetera.

RINDLESS AND CANNED CHEESES

The function of a cheese's rind is to protect the interior of the cheese so that it can ripen and develop harmoniously. A well closed, firm, natural rind keeps the cheese in shape and makes it practically impossible for anything undesirable from outside to penetrate. On bloomy and washed rind cheeses the degree of bacterial activity which takes place on and in the rind affects the final flavour of the interior of the cheese.

Rindless cheeses are basically a packaging and marketing asset for the manufacturer. What happens is that after a cheese is formed and salted, it is sealed in a plastic wrapping or film in which the cheese ripens and in which it is often marketed. No rind forms on the cheese, the plastic doing the job of protecting the cheese.

The savings to the manufacturer on this type of cheese are obvious; from the consumer's viewpoint the cheese will keep longer when kept in its plastic wrapper and there is no wastage of cheese (no rind to cut away). But as there is no rind there is a loss in flavour. Rindless cheeses are milder and blander tasting; they lack depth, individuality and intensity of flavour because the rind which helps create such things does not exist.

Should rinds be eaten with a cheese or cut away? Certain cheeses have hard, tough rinds which are obviously not designed to be eaten and will have to be removed. But with cheeses like Brie and Camembert and numerous other bloomy and washed rind types this is not the case. Indeed, many people find the rind on a Camembert or Brie 'the best part'.

Nevertheless, there are several lofty authorities on the subject who insist that the rind should be removed from any cheese, regardless of type, to appreciate the true flavour. The man or woman who does this with every cheese encountered can be considered either a true connoisseur or someone with the fastidious eating habits of a sixteenth century Spanish grandee.

Canned Camemberts and Bries are a fairly popular feature of the cheese market today. Of these it should be said that their major advantage is that they can be stored almost indefinitely, but in taste they are a long way from fresh Camembert or Brie. Any food that is packaged in cans has to be subjected to heat treatment to prevent it deteriorating. In effect, a canned cheese has been pasteurised (not just the milk from which the cheese has been made, but the cheese itself). Such a cheese can never have the quality, subtlety and depth of flavour of a natural cheese. At best a useful standby and relatively economical compared to the price of fresh Brie or Camembert—but not to be compared to the two great classic cheeses of France.

A word too about the composition of this book. Cheeses are listed in alphabetical order. Those that the average cheese buyer is likely to come across are described in considerable detail, as are others that are unusual or interesting. Besides a description of the cheese, its fat content is given, wines which will complement it are suggested, along with serving tips. The type or group to which the cheese belongs is also detailed and each cheese's aroma is broadly defined as 'pronounced' or 'unpronounced'. When a cheese has an interesting background or story associated with it, this is mentioned. Related cheeses are described more briefly to avoid repetition, and cross-referenced to the cheese to which they are similar.

Dimensions and shapes of individual cheeses and individual brands vary so widely that the dimensions given throughout the book are intended only as a reference to the general size and shape.

Finally, it should be stressed that a cheese purchased outside its country of origin will often taste stronger than one purchased within its country of origin. This is because the cheese will have spent time travelling and in storage. It will have continued to age and develop and thus have gained in strength of flavour.

CHEESE LANGUAGE

Like wine, there is a variety of expressions used in regard to cheese which can cause confusion. The language of the world of cheese can be surrounded by as much mystique, nonsense and pretension as that of wine. This shouldn't be so, of course, and the descriptive terms in this book have been kept as basic as possible.

The following glossary defines expressions used in the book with which some readers might not be familiar and others that might be encountered outside of its pages.

Acid, acidulous: a term used to describe a cheese with a lightly sourish flavour.

Ammoniated, ammoniacal: when certain cheeses are past their prime and overripe they will smell and often taste of ammonia. This particularly applies to soft cheeses such as Brie and Camembert. For those unfamiliar with this smell, it can possibly best be described by imagining a cheese that has been sprayed by a particularly virulent tom cat—a thing to be avoided at all costs!

Annatto: a colouring agent used to colour a great variety of cheeses ranging from English Cheddar to the French Maroilles. Annatto is a dye obtained from a South American plant.

Aroma: a cheese's smell or odour which can vary from lightly aromatic to ferociously overpowering. Note that while most strong smelling cheese will also be strong tasting, this does not apply to all. Limburger is a case in point. The American cheeses Brick and Liederkranz both have distinctive aromas but are not overly strong tasting cheeses unless well aged.

Barnyardy: a descriptive term often used to describe a cheese's aroma and sometimes its taste as well. Many people find goat's milk cheeses barnyardy, particularly aged ones.

Bleu: French name for blue veined cheeses.

Bloomy rind: cheeses that develop a light white down on their surfaces are known as bloomy or flowery rind cheeses. Such a rind develops as a result of the cheese's surface being sprayed with the *Penicillium candidum* spore. The best known cheeses of this type are Camembert and Brie.

Brushed: certain types of natural rind cheeses, cooked and uncooked varieties, have their rinds brushed during the period they spend ripening. This brushing, done by hand or machine, helps the interior of the cheese to keep moist during the ripening period; it also has an effect on the final flavour of the cheese.

Casein: the element of milk which solidifies when coagulation takes place.

Cellar: the room, usually underground, where cheeses are left to ripen. Some cheeses, Roquefort is the most famous, are ripened in caves.

Cheddaring: a cheese that is 'cheddared' has its curd cut into blocks which are turned and stacked at the bottom of the cheese vat at intervals of ten to fifteen minutes for about one-and-a-half hours.

Close: used to describe a cheese's texture. A close textured cheese is one which is smooth, unblemished and devoid of holes or cracks.

Cooked: a step in the cheesemaking process when the cheese curd is heated, sometimes in the surplus whey. Cooked cheeses are all hard cheeses such as Emmentaler and other Swiss types.

Cream: the fatty element of milk.

Creamy: used to describe both the taste and sometimes the texture of certain cheeses.

Curdling: an early stage in cheesemaking when milk coagulates due to the introduction of rennet.

Curing: also known as maturing or ageing— the stage in the cheesemaking process when a cheese is left to ripen.

Crumbly: the condition of a cheese that breaks away when cut—often applicable to blue veins.

Dry matter: the part of the cheese that remains after all moisture is removed. Soft cheeses, such as Brie and Camembert, will, on average, contain about 50 per cent dry matter and 50 per cent water.

Earthy: a descriptive term often used to describe the nature of monastery cheeses.

Fat content: the fat content of cheese refers to the fat content in the dry matter of the cheese. It is usually indicated on the cheese's packaging. The average is 45 per cent but it can be as low as 4 per cent and as high as 75 per cent.

Formaggio: Italian for cheese.

Fresh cheese: a cheese that does not undergo a ripening period—e.g. Cottage Cheese, Cream Cheese, Ricotta.

Fromage: French for cheese.

Gruyère: not only the name of one of the best known Swiss cheeses in the world but also a general name for large cheeses made in France —e.g. Gruyère de Comte, Beaufort, Emmentaler.

Hard: descriptive term for cooked cheeses.

Holes: also called 'eyes', basically openings in the body of cheeses such as Emmentaler, Gruyère and other Swiss types. Such holes are spherical, equally spaced and about the size of cherry stones. The holes are caused by bacterial activity which generates prioponic acid causing gas to expand within the curd.

Kaas: Dutch for cheese.

Käse: German for cheese.

Lactic: milk aroma, sometimes flavour, of certain cheeses.

Micro-organisms: yeasts and ferments present in milk and milk curd.

Monastery: certain cheeses are linked historically in that they were originally developed by monks. They are known as monastery cheeses although they range in flavour and aroma considerably.

Moulds: moulds can be on the surface of cheese or be developed internally. Surface moulds are the result of cheese being treated with the *Penicillium candidum* spore; internal moulds are created by the introduction of *Penicillium glaucum* or *Penicillium roqueforti* spores both to create blue veined cheeses. Certain French goat milk cheeses develop a natural bluish surface mould and some of the newer double crème cheeses have both a surface mould and an internal mould—e.g. Blue Castello, Bavarian Blue, Duet.

Mushroomy: flavour and aroma description of certain soft and semi-soft cheeses, particularly members of the Brie/Camembert family.

Nutty: flavour description of certain cheeses, often refers to a hazelnut flavour.

Open: texture description referring to a cheese which contains openings and holes in its body. The opposite of *close.*

Paraffined: many cheeses are coated with a paraffin wax, particularly those destined for export markets. Edam is probably the best known. The wax protects the cheese.

Pasteurisation: the treatment given to partially sterilised milk.

Paste: the interior of a cheese.

Pronounced: descriptive term for a cheese's aroma or flavour.

Penicillium: moulds that are developed on the surface of bloomy rind cheeses (Camembert, Brie) and internally in blue veins (see *moulds*).

Persille: a French term for a blue vein cheese used in reference to Roquefort because it is the only bleu from sheep's milk.

Piquant: descriptive term for a sharp tasting cheese.

Rennet: a substance obtained from the stomach linings of young calves which contains a coagulating enzyme.

Rind: the protective external surface of a cheese. Rinds can be natural or artificially created, thick or thin, hard or soft, washed, oiled, brushed or paraffined. Their prime role is to protect the cheese's interior and allow it to ripen and develop harmoniously. Their presence affects the final flavour of the interior of the cheese.

Skimmed milk: when part or all of the cream has been removed from milk, the milk is referred to as skimmed. Cheeses made from such milk generally have a lower fat content than average; some (but not all) are quite pronounced in taste.

Starter: a bacterial culture which produces lactic acid.

Supple: descriptive term used to describe a cheese's texture—firm but not hard, pliable and resilient.

Tangy: descriptive term used to denote a cheese's flavour usually meaning sharp, distinctive, flavoursome.

Texture: a cheese's texture can be soft, firm, hard, semi-soft, supple, waxy, open, close and so on. Texture is largely dependent on its moisture content—the softer the cheese the higher its moisture content.

Washed rind cheeses: the rinds of certain cheeses are regularly washed while they are being ripened. The purpose of this is to keep the cheese moist, supple and to ensure it does not dry out. Such washings can be done with elements as varied as salt water or brandy—thus the washing plays a part in the cheese's final flavour. Some of the strongest smelling and tasting cheeses in the world are washed rind varieties.

CHEESES A TO Z

ALLGAU EMMENTALER

A German version of Emmentaler made in 98 kg (220 lb) sizes, matured up to eight months.
(See *Emmentaler*.)

ALPKASE

A type of German Emmentaler made in the High Alps. The cheese is also known as Bergkäse.
(See *Emmentaler*.)

ALTAPOL

Country of origin: Australia.

Background: This is a new cheese with a higher than normal level of polyunsaturated fats. The cheese was developed by the Australian Commonwealth Scientific and Industrial Research Organisation and is now marketed by a commercial company. According to the manufacturers, milk usually has a polyunsaturated fat level of three per cent. Altapol has a polyunsaturated fat level of 20 per cent.

The cheese was developed in view of mounting evidence from heart research implicating saturated fats with cardiovascular illness. It is a cheese obviously suitable for anyone with a heart condition or merely concerned with fat intake.

Description: Altapol is a Cheddar style cheese, light yellow in colour with a firm, close texture. It is marketed in 5 kg (11¼ lb) rindless blocks. Processed and smoked process versions are also produced in 250 g (8 oz) packs.

Altapol has a pleasant Cheddar taste, undemanding but not unattractive with a mildish tangy bite.

Wines: Light reds and whites.
Serve: Snacks; sandwiches.
Fat content: 34 per cent.
Aroma: Unpronounced.
Type: Cheddar.

ALTESSE

A French double crème, creamy, rich but essentially mild tasting. The cheese has a 60 per cent fat content and is marketed in a square cardboard box weighing approximately 210 g (7 oz). Used chiefly as a dessert cheese, it goes well with fruit or French bread. The cheese is easily spreadable once it has reached room temperature.
(See *Double Crèmes*.)

AMBROSIA

Country of origin: Sweden.

Description: A popular, widely marketed Swedish cheese usually produced in wheel shapes some 25 cm (10 in) in diameter and some 10 cm (4 in) deep. It has a waxed rind.

The cheese is made from cow's milk and ripened for about two months. It has a semisoft rather waxy texture, is a light yellow in colour and has a series of small holes and splits across the interior paste. In taste Ambrosia is smooth, creamy and buttery but with a faintly sourish tinge, rather like a very mild Esrom.

Wines: Dry whites, light reds.
Serve: End of meals, snacks.
Fat content: 45 per cent.
Type: Monastery/mild.
Aroma: Unpronounced.

AMERICAN EDAM

Mild, bland and buttery and usually made in loaf shapes. These cheeses are often made in small sizes weighing from 360 g ($\frac{3}{4}$ lb) to 500 g (1 lb). They are all, of course, modelled on the famous Dutch cheese.
(See *Edam.*)

AMERICAN EMMENTALER

This cheese is also known as Swiss and sometimes Schweizer or Sweitzer. The cheese is ripened for three to four months; it has the correct balance of sweetness and nuttiness but is less pronounced in taste than the Swiss cheese on which it is based. American Swiss has been produced domestically since the middle of last century. Most comes from Illinois and Wisconsin.
(See *Emmentaler.*)

ANCHOR

A medium-strong New Zealand Cheddar.
(See *Cheddar.*)

ANFROM

A variety of Oka, the Canadian cheese produced in Quebec by Trappist monks, which itself is modelled on Port Salut. Anfrom is another Canadian variety of this cheese, mellow to robust in flavour depending on age. It is made in small disc shapes with a russet coloured, thin washed rind and a yellow, semi-soft creamy interior.
(See *Port Salut* and *Oka.*)

APPENZELL

Country of origin: Switzerland.

Background: This cheese takes its name from the Canton of Appenzell. It is made in a similar fashion to Emmentaler, being a cooked, pressed cheese. Appenzell is an historic Swiss cheese, some authorities dating it back to the days of Charlemagne (A.D. 742-814).

Description: Appenzell is made in the shape of a small wheel 35 cm (14 in) in diameter and 7.5 cm (3 in) thick. It is a hard, firm-textured cheese with a brownish natural rind. The interior is yellow and lightly dotted with pea-sized holes. Before the cheese undergoes its three to six-month ripening period, it is immersed for up to a week in cider or white wine and treated with various spices. When young, Appenzell is a rather delicate, fragrant flavoured cheese with a distinctive but pleasant aroma. Older cheeses, which include most cheeses bought outside Switzerland, are more pronounced in taste and smell, rather like a stronger-tasting Gruyère.

Appenzell Rass is a more full-blooded relation. It is made from skimmed milk instead of whole cow's milk like Appenzell. It shares most of the physical characteristics of Appenzell but is put into a mixture of white wine, cider and spices for several weeks, sometimes months. This makes for a very pungent, spicy and tangy flavoured cheese. *Rass*, in fact, means 'sharp'.

Wines: Light reds and whites for Appenzell; stronger, full-bodied reds for Appenzell Rass.
Serve: Appenzell goes well with fresh fruit salad or raw vegetables, with nuts or with fruits such as pears, apples, grapes and fresh figs.
Fat content: Appenzell 45 per cent; Appenzell Rass 20 per cent.
Type: Swiss.
Aroma: Distinctive when young; strong and pungent when well matured.

ASIAGO

Country of origin: Italy.

Background: One of the numerous Italian Grana style cheeses which date back to A.D. 1200. Asiago originally came from the plateau of Asiago in the province of Vicenza and is a relative newcomer to the family, having been created in the last half of the nineteenth century.

Description: Asiago is a hard, pressed, semi-cooked cow's milk cheese which, depending on how long it has been aged, can be used as a table or a grating cheese. The cheese is made in the shape of a small wheel 45 cm (18 in) in diameter and 12.5 cm (5 in) thick. Asiago has a smooth glossy rind and is firm-textured, with a series of small holes of different sizes scattered across its interior. The cheese is light yellow in colour.

Aged up to twelve months, it is a sharp, tangy, flaky (but not crumbly) cheese with a bite somewhat like Cheddar. Aged past twelve months the cheese becomes extremely hard, brittle and granular in texture. It has little aroma but is quite sharp and pronounced to the taste.

Wines: Fruity reds for young cheeses.
Serve: When young, Asiago is a good all round table cheese with 'bite', suitable for sandwiches and snacks; aged Asiagos make excellent grating cheeses and are used in a similar fashion to Parmesan.
Fat content: 30-45 per cent.
Type: Extra-hard grating cheese/Cheddar.
Aroma: Unpronounced.

AUSTRALIAN EDAM

Australia produces several versions of Edam in different areas including western Victoria, the north-west coast of Tasmania, north-east of Adelaide and Toowoomba, Queensland. The cheese is mild and bland with a smooth resilient texture. As well as being produced in the traditional ball shape, it is made in pre-packaged blocks.
(See *Edam*.)

AUSTRALIAN EMMENTALER

A copy of the famous Swiss cheese, it is matured for only three to four months, has a rather more rubbery texture and is a paler yellow. It is quite sweet and nutlike, but not as distinctive and complex as the Swiss cheese. In Australia it is often called Swiss cheese.
(See *Emmentaler*.)

AUSTRALIAN GOUDA

Several types are made based on the Dutch original—they are usually mild, bland, firm textured, buttery cheeses.
(See *Gouda*.)

AUSTRALIAN GRUYERE

This version of the Swiss cheese is close textured, lacking holes although it sometimes has a few cracks. Nutty, faintly sweetish in taste, pleasant but bland and uninteresting compared to the Swiss variety, lacking that cheese's complexity of flavour and distinction.
(See *Gruyère*.)

AUSTRIAN EMMENTALER

There are two types; one made as a baby Emmentaler weighing 40 kg (90 lb) which is soft and delicate with a sweet nutty flavour and quite a dry texture; a larger version is stronger flavoured with a firmer texture.
(See *Emmentaler*.)

AUSTRIAN GRUYERE

A copy of the Swiss cheese, rather drier in texture more salty and with a harder rind.
(See *Gruyère*.)

BABYBEL

A smaller version of the French cheese Bonbel. The cheese is marketed in a red wax coating in 200 g (7 oz) sizes. Essentially it is an extremely mild, bland Port Salut style cheese.
(See *Bonbel*.)

BABY EDAM

This is a small sized version of the Dutch cheese Edam. It is made in ball shapes weighing between 880 g and 1100 g (2-2¼ lb).
(See *Edam*.)

BABY GOUDA

A small sized version of Gouda made in weights varying from 300 g (10 oz) to 600 g (20 oz).
(See *Gouda*.)

BACKSTEINER

A German cheese similar to Limburger. Although the name means 'brick' (referring to its shape) the cheese bears no relation to the American Brick cheese.
(See *Limburger*.)

BACON FLAVOURED CHEDDAR

This is an unusual variety of Australian Cheddar produced in Queensland. The cheese was created at the Caboolture Co-operative Association, north of Brisbane. Because of the abundance of local ham suppliers on the nearby Darling Downs, the cheese is actually studded with pieces of ham, cooked and prepared by the cheesemaker himself. The Cheddar is semi-mature, with a distinct smoky flavour and is packed in 250 g (8 oz), 500 g (1 lb) and 1 kg (2¼ lb) packs.
(See *Cheddar*.)

BAGOZZO

An Italian grating cheese belonging to the Grana style of cheeses, the best known of which is Parmesan.
(See *Grana* and *Parmesan*.)

BANON

Country of origin: France.

Description: This goat's milk cheese is made in a small disc shape measuring about 7.5 cm (3 in) in diameter and 2.5 cm (1 in) thick. It is a soft cheese with a natural rind, slightly sticky. The firm-textured supple interior is creamy white in colour. During its making process the cheese is dipped in a mixture of brandy and a juice extracted from grape skins. It then undergoes a maturing process in stone jugs for two months. It is then packaged wrapped in chestnut leaves tied with raffia.

Younger Banons, aged about two weeks, are mild, fragrant cheeses with a slight tinge of hazelnut flavour. The older cheeses gain considerably in flavour as they age—at two months they can be quite strong. Banon is sometimes made from sheep's or cow's milk.

Banon au Pèbre d'Ai, a variety flavoured with herbs, is also known as Poivre d'Ane.

Wines: If served alone, dry whites such as rieslings or hocks; if eaten with fruits, serve fuller whites such as traminers, spätleses or hermitages.
Serve: End of meals.
Fat content: 45 per cent.
Type: Goat's milk cheese.
Aroma: Unpronounced when young; aged versions quite pungent.

BARAKA

This is a Camembert-style cheese made in the shape of a horse-shoe. The cheese has the familiar white, downy rind Camembert appearance; in taste quite mild.
(See *Camembert*.)

BAUERHAND

The name means 'peasant hand' and the cheese is part of the range of German sour curd cheeses. While low in fat content and high in protein value, such cheeses are very distinctive

25

in flavour and aroma—often, particularly with well aged versions, overpoweringly so.
(See *Sour Curd Cheeses*, *Harz* and *Mainz*.)

BAVARIAN BLUE

Country of origin: Germany.

Background: One of the new versions of double crème cheeses that combine a white moulded surface with a blue veined interior.

Description: Bavarian Blue is made in small wheel shapes measuring approximately 25 cm (10 in) in diameter and 5 cm (2 in) thick. The cheese, made from cow's milk enriched with cream, is a combination of a white moulded surface, blue veining and a double crème content. This results in a very rich, creamy, soft-textured cheese, easily spreadable. The blue vein flavouring is quite mild but sufficient to give a pleasantly sourish tang which admirably offsets the cheese's lush richness. As the cheese ages its white mould becomes brown in colour and the cheese develops quite a sharp taste. As with all double crème and triple crème cheeses, Bavarian Blue does not have a long life and should be eaten within a relatively short time of purchase.

Wines: Light reds; dry whites.
Serve: End of meals with French bread; snacks.
Fat content: 70 per cent.
Type: Double crème/blue vein.
Aroma: Unpronounced, apart from a light mould smell and creamy freshness.

BAYERNLAND

A German range of processed cheese.
(See *Processed Cheese*.)

BEAUFORT

Country of origin: France.

Background: An ancient French cheese dating back centuries which is akin to Swiss Gruyère.

The cheese is also known as Gruyère de Beaufort and is thought to have been known to the ancient Romans.

Description: Like Gruyère, this is a pressed, cooked cow's milk cheese made in the shape of a large millstone up to 60 cm (24 in) in diameter and 12.5 cm (5 in) thick. Some of these huge cheeses can weigh up to 70 kg (157 lb). Beaufort is a hard cheese which is matured for a minimum period of six months. Its dry, tough, naturally-formed rind is greyish-gold in colour and its yellow interior is firm but supple feeling. Unlike Gruyère, the interior is smooth and not dotted with holes or 'eyes'. (These holes or eyes only appear in cooked cheeses which are fermented and ripened in warm cellars, causing gas or air bubbles to develop in the cheese's curd.) Beaufort ripens in a cooler atmosphere, which slows down bacterial activity.

In flavour, Beaufort can be compared to Gruyère, although it is richer, fuller, more buttery tasting.

Wines: Fruity reds and whites.
Serve: End of meals.
Fat content: 50 per cent.
Type: Swiss.
Aroma: Unpronounced.

BEAUMONT

Country of origin: France.

Background: This cheese comes from the Savoy region and is similar in style to Trappist type cheeses.

Description: Beaumont is a pressed, uncooked cheese, semi-soft in texture. It is made from cow's milk. The cheese has a light yellow rind, quite supple-feeling, and an ivory-white interior paste. It is made in disc shapes 20 cm (8 in) in diameter and 5 cm (2 in) thick.

The cheese is ripened for about six weeks. In taste quite pleasant—mild, creamy but with an earthy quality similar to monastery cheeses such as Reblochon and Oka.

Wines: Full, grape-flavoured red wines.
Serve: End of meals.

Fat content: 50 per cent.
Type: Monastery.
Aroma: Unpronounced.

BEAU PASTEUR

A French range of processed cheese.
(See *Processed Cheese*.)

BEER CHEESE

A square shaped German cheese made from a mixture of skimmed and whole cow's milk also known as Bierkäse and Weisslacker. The cheese is both strong smelling and strong tasting; the Germans eat this cheese with and sometimes *in* beer.
(See *Weisslacker*.)

BEGA

(See Australian *Cheddars*.)

BEGUIN

A French processed cheese (fromage fondu) which is also a double crème cheese. Beguin is flavoured with walnuts—rich, smooth, creamy with a very distinctive walnut tang.
(See *Processed Cheese*.)

BELLE BRESSANE

A soft, creamy French blue vein with a white downy crust, made in the shape of a small wheel with the centre cut out. The cheese comes from Grièges and is a rich, creamy tasting blue vein rather than a strong pungent one, similar in taste to Bresse Bleu and Pipo Crem'.
(See *Pipo Crem'* and *Bresse Bleu*.)

BELLELAYE

Country of origin: Switzerland.

Background: Bellelaye, which comes from the canton of Berne, is an ancient cheese which dates back to the fifteenth century. It is also known as Tête de Moine. At the monastery of Bellelaye where the cheese originated it was the practice for each monk to receive a regular ration of one whole cheese.

Description: Bellelaye is made in the shape of a small cylinder 12.5 cm (5 in) in diameter and 12.5 cm high. It is a pressed, uncooked cheese made from cow's milk and ripened for a minimum period of three months. The rind is slightly tacky, yellowish in colour, and masks a smooth, close, firm-textured supple interior, white to yellow. The cheese has a noticeable fruity aroma and is full-flavoured, spicy and tangy.

Wines: Fruity red wines.
Serve: End of meals.
Fat content: 45-50 per cent.
Type: Swiss/monastery.
Aroma: Noticeable, fruity, not unpleasant.

BELLETOILE

A French triple crème—a cheese with a 72-75 per cent fat content.
(See *Triple Crèmes*.)

BEL PAESE

Country of origin: Italy.

Background: The name means 'beautiful country', and refers to the Lombardy area of Italy where the cheese first appeared around 1920. Soft, creamy cheeses of this type have been produced in Italy for more than sixty years. Bel Paese is the most famous but others of the type include Bel Piano Lombardo, Cacioreale, Bella Milano, Bella Alpina, Pastorello, Savoia and Vittoria.

Other European countries and the USA also make copies of this cheese but none is in the

same class as the Italian. The Italian cheese can be identified by its foil wrapper which depicts a priest against a background of a map of Italy (the wrapping on the American version looks similar but the map is of North and South America).

Description: Bel Paese is a soft textured cheese made in the shape of a disc measuring 20 cm (8 in) in diameter and about 5 cm (2 in) thick. The cheese has the consistency of firm butter, is a pale cream colour, free of holes, and virtually odourless apart from a very light milky aroma. In flavour the cheese is mild, but delicately rich, sweet and creamy; at its best rated as one of Italy's finest soft cheeses.

Bel Paese is a fast ripening cheese which is matured for six to eight weeks before it is ready for marketing.

Wines: Light whites, rosés.
Serve: End of meals; snacks; with fruit.
Fat content: 45-50 per cent.
Type: Bland/buttery.
Aroma: Unpronounced.

BERGKASE

The name means 'mountain cheese' and it is made in the German High Alps. Bergkäse is also known as 'Alpkäse'. It is a type of Emmentaler.
(See *Emmentaler*.)

BIAROM

A German version of Danish Esrom, sometimes known as German Port du Salut. A mild version of this style of cheese but rich, buttery and pleasant tasting.
(See *Port Salut*.)

BITTO

An Italian Swiss style cheese which can be made from cow's milk, sheep's milk or a mixture of goat's and cow's milk. Skimmed milk varieties are also made. It is used as a table cheese when made from whole milk and is similar to the more famous Fontina; when matured for periods up to two years and made from skimmed milk it is used as a grating cheese.
(See *Fontina*.)

BJELKE BLUE

Despite its name, not a blue veined cheese but a mild flavoured Australian Cheddar studded with peanuts throughout its body. It is named in honour of Mr Bjelke-Petersen, state premier of Queensland and a successful peanut farmer.
(See *Cheddar*.)

BLACK DIAMOND

An extremely highly rated Canadian Cheddar which is made from unpasteurised cow's milk.
(See Canadian *Cheddars*.)

BLACK WAX

(See American *Cheddars*.)

BLEU DE BRESSE

Country of origin: France.

Background: A relatively new French blue vein, now quite popular. Created in 1950, it was originally modelled on the Italian Gorgonzola. The cheese is also known as Bresse Bleu.

Description: The cheese is made in cylinder shapes as small as 6.5 cm (2½ in) in diameter and 4 cm (1½ in) thick; it comes foil wrapped in a cardboard box. It has a thin yellow-whitish rind often speckled with brownish pigmentation. The interior of the cheese is soft, spreadable, whitish in colour and tinged with streaks of blue veining. To the taste it is a rich, creamy blue vein, savoury and full flavoured rather than sharp and penetrating.

The cheese is made from cow's milk and dependent on its size is matured for up to three months. Past its prime the cheese quickly becomes over-strong and gamy in both flavour and aroma; it is advisable to eat it within a few days of purchase. At its best a blue vein with a deservedly high reputation.

Wines: Full, rich red wines.
Serve: End of meals with crusty French bread.
Fat content: 50 per cent.
Type: Blue Vein.
Aroma: Mould smell, not overpronounced.

BLEU DU HAUT JURA

Country of origin: France.

Background: This is a well rated French blue produced high in the Jura Mountains. It is also known as Bleu de Gex or Bleu de Septmoncel.

Description: The cheese is made in disc shapes some 30 cm (12 in) across and 9 cm (3½ in) thick. It has a smooth grey rind, a fine, close, soft texture, white with well distributed blue veining. The cheese has a distinctive tang; it is savoury, fulsome, somewhat bitter but a blue vein of quality and distinction. It is made from cow's milk and is matured for up to three months.

Wines: Full flavoured reds.
Serve: End of meals with French bread.
Fat content: 45 per cent.
Type: Blue Vein.
Aroma: Unpronounced.

BLEUS

Country of origin: France.

Description: *Bleu* is a name given to all French blue-veined cheeses—cheeses with an internal blue mould. There are two types: one having a naturally-formed dry rind and the other having virtually no rind or one so thin as to be almost transparent, and whose surface is rather sticky or tacky.

The rind of the former is brushed during the curing process; the latter is subjected to continual brushings and scrapings so that the rind is thinned down and worn away.

Cheeses in the first category include Bleu de Corse (a blue vein from Corsica modelled on Roquefort), Bleu de Gex (quite a strong tasting cheese whose rind turns brown with age), Bleu de Septmoncel, Bleu de Sassenage and Fourme d'Ambert. Cheeses in the second category include Bleu d'Auvergne, Bleu des Causses, Bleu de Laqueuille, Bleu de Quercy, Saingorlon and Bleu de Bresse.

The most notable French bleu is Roquefort, which differs from the rest in that it is made from ewe's milk as opposed to cow's milk.

Most French blue veins are strong, pungent and tangy tasting cheeses. The best are those where the veining is thick and well distributed. Nearly all are treated with the *Penicillium glaucum* spore; the exception is Roquefort which is injected with a spore called *Penicillium roqueforti* developed in rye bread. Bleus are usually made in thick discs or cylindrical shapes.

Serve: End of meals; crumbled into salads.
Wines: Strong, hearty reds.
Fat content: 45-50 per cent.
Type: Blue veins.
Aroma: Noticeably pungent.

BLUE CASTELLO

Country of origin: Denmark.

Background: A double crème cheese with blue veining which is related to Crema Dania. The cheese is also known as Blå Castello.

Description: Blue Castello comes packaged in a blue-and-white half-decagonal shaped box in 140 g (4½ oz) weights. Made from cow's milk enriched with cream, the cheese has a brownish-white surface mould, a double-crème content and blue veining. Blue Castello has a creamily soft texture, easily spreadable, and a pure white interior speckled with blue veining. The blue vein flavour is mild but sufficient to add a pleasant tanginess to the exceptionally rich, voluptuously creamy flavour of the cheese.

Blue Castello is ripened for up to three weeks, when it develops its light bloomy rind.

Bavarian Blue (top), Blue Castello (below)

Like all double crèmes (due to its very high fat content it can almost be classed as a triple crème) it does not have a long life and when purchased should be eaten within days.

Wines: Fruity red wines.
Serve: End of meals with fresh crusty bread; goes well with fruits such as strawberries, grapes and ripe pears.
Fat content: 70 per cent.
Type: Double crème/blue vein.
Aroma: Light mould aroma, not overpronounced.

BLUE CHESHIRE

A Cheshire cheese that formerly developed a blue veining quite spontaneously. This is a highly rated English blue vein, on a par with Stilton. Today many Blue Cheshires acquire their veining by artificial inoculation. (See *Cheshire*.)

BLUE VEINS

Blue-veined cheese is made by all the major cheese producing countries in the world. The three best known—and most highly regarded —are the French Roquefort, the English Stilton and the Italian Gorgonzola. However, there are numerous other varieties, many of them excellent cheeses.

Blue veins are so called because of the distinctive pattern of veining that streaks their interiors. This is usually blue or blue-black but it can be greenish, as in the case of Gorgonzola. The veins originally developed accidentally, but today are the result of treatment with *Penicillium* spores.

During their ripening period the cheeses are perforated by special needles—this allows air to enter the body of the cheese and promotes the growth of a blue mould. The process takes place in cellars or curing chambers with a high degree of humidity. Blue veins thus differ from other types of cheese in that they ripen from the inside instead of from the outside.

They are classed as soft cheeses, are often crumbly and are characterised by a strong, tangy, pungent flavour and often aroma.

The following is a comparison of several popular brands. The majority of these are treated in detail elsewhere in the book.

BAVARIAN BLUE (Germany): A cheese that is a combination of moulded surface, blue veining and an extra high fat content. A very lush, rich, creamy cheese with a mildly sourish tang. The blue vein flavour is mild, but the cheese's high fat content almost makes it a triple crème.
Fat content: 70 per cent.

BLEU D'AUVERGNE (France): A stronger flavoured cheese which was developed as a copy of Roquefort, made from cow's milk. The cheese has a thin yellowish-brown rind, a pungent aroma and a sharp and distinctive taste.
Fat content: 45 per cent.

BLEU DE BRESSE (France): A well regarded French bleu, rich, creamy, soft-textured and savoury. Full-flavoured but not over-sharp or pronounced in taste.
Fat content: 50 per cent.

BLEU DE GEX, also known as Bleu du Haut Jura and Septmoncel (France): Another quality French bleu with a naturally formed greyish rind which turns brown with age. Full flavoured and tangy.
Fat content: 45 per cent.

BLEU DES CAUSSES (France): Like d'Auvergne, a strong, full-flavoured cheese, rich and creamy.
Fat content: 45 per cent.

BLUE CASTELLO (Denmark): This cheese has a moulded surface, blue veining and a high fat content. Rich, creamy and luscious but essentially mild in its flavouring. A similar cheese to Bavarian Blue.
Fat content: 70 per cent.

BOLINA (Denmark): Bolina is similar to Gorgonzola but not as creamy or as strong tasting.
Fat content: 50 per cent.

Danish Blue Vein Cheeses: Danablu (top), Mycella (left), Bolina (right)

DANABLU (Denmark): A fine, rather crumbly cheese with a buttery consistency. Its saltiness is offset by an almost peppermint-like sharp flavour.
Fat content: 50 per cent.

DUET (Denmark): Another cheese in the *genre* of Blue Castello and Bavarian Blue, a cheese with a moulded surface, blue veining and a high fat content. Extremely rich, creamy and buttery to the taste with a mild blue vein flavour.
Fat content: 70 per cent.

ERBO (Italy): An extremely mild-flavoured blue vein and for a very good reason—it is a processed cheese (the makers state that the cheese is made from a mixture of processed cheese and blue moulded cheese). Quite popular with people who find natural blue-veined cheeses too strong.
Fat content: 40 per cent.

FOURME D'AMBERT (France): Quite a pronounced tasting French bleu with a distinctive 'bite', sometimes rather bitter.
Fat content: 45 per cent.

GERMAN BLUE VEIN: A well-balanced cheese, soft, creamy and piquant but not over pronounced in taste or saltiness.
Fat content: 50 per cent.

GORGONZOLA (Italy): One of the world's top blue veins, although its veining is greenish rather than blue. Rich, succulent and creamier and softer than its two rivals, Stilton and Roquefort, it is still strong and pungent in both flavour and aroma.
Fat content: 48 per cent.

MYCELLA (Denmark): A copy of Gorgonzola with greenish rather than blue veining. Stronger tasting than Danablu but creamy and rich rather than oversharp. The cheese has the full flavour of Gorgonzola but not the complexity or the soft texture.
Fat content: 50 per cent.

NEW ZEALAND BLUE: A dry crumbly cheese, rather sharp, with pronounced saltiness.
Fat content: 50 per cent.

NORWEGIAN BLUE: A cheese based on Roquefort but made from cow's milk. Held in quite high esteem, well blended, tangy and piquant.
Fat content: 50 per cent.

PIPO CREM' (France): An extremely popular French cheese, milder than most but rich, creamy and well-blended with no over-pronounced harshness or saltiness in its flavour. The cheese is related to Bleu de Bresse and is produced in long cylinders about 12.5 cm (5 in) in diameter.
Fat content: 50 per cent.

ROQUEFORT (France): The oldest known blue vein in the world and one which was enjoyed by the Romans. It is the only blue vein detailed here made from sheep's milk. Totally distinctive in taste, rich and creamy, but often, particularly in cheeses bought outside France, with a marked saltiness in its flavour.
Fat content: 45 per cent.

STILTON (England): The classic English blue, strong-flavoured, distinctive, a cheese that combines the pungent, tangy, blue vein flavour with clean Cheddar undertones. Full-bodied but mellow with a rather pebbly consistency.
Fat content: 55 per cent.

UNITY BLUE (Australia): Made in 2 kg (4½ lb) wheels and 125 g (¼ lb) foil wrapped wedges, this is the only blue vein cheese produced in Australia. Made in Queensland, it is quite a sharp, tangy blue.
Fat content: 48-50 per cent.

BLUE VINNY

Country of origin: Great Britain (England).

Background: This cheese is also known as Dorset Blue. It is quite a famous and somewhat mysterious old English cheese that is scarcely seen nowadays. It is believed to have been a favourite of the West Country writer Thomas Hardy. The name is derived from the fact that it is a blue vein and an old West Country word *vinew*, which means 'mould'.

Unity Blue (top), Norwegian Blue (below)

Description: Blue Vinny is a cylindrical cheese standing some 15 cm (6 in) high and 20 cm (8 in) in diameter. Made from skimmed cow's milk, it is a blue veined cheese which develops a single blue streak, rather than a network of veins. The cheese has a noticeable aroma and a sharp pronounced flavour, somewhat salty.

Blue Vinny is matured for up to six months and needs to be eaten fairly promptly, as it is notorious for hardening very quickly once it ages past its prime.

This cheese virtually disappeared from sight when English health regulations decreed that cheesemaking could not take place in buildings where animals were kept. To develop the blue mould in the cheese, the old cheesemakers used to dip horse bridles into the milk. The micro-organisms on the bridles started the mould.

Blue Vinny is now being made again and produced under more controlled conditions, but is still quite rare.

Wines: Full-bodied reds.
Serve: End of meals.
Fat content: Up to 28 per cent.
Type: Blue vein.
Aroma: Noticeable smell of mould.

BODALLA

(See Australian *Cheddars*.)

BOLINA

A Danish blue vein modelled on Gorgonzola. (See *Blue Veins*.)

BONBEL

Country of origin: France.

Background: Bonbel, of fairly recent origin, is a brand name for yet another version of Saint Paulin.

Description: Bonbel is made in disc shapes some 5 cm (2 in) thick and 23 cm (9 in) in diameter. It is a cow's milk cheese which is ripened for two months. Bonbel is light yellow in colour with a smooth, supple-feeling texture and rind. In flavour it could be said to be a mild-mannered Saint Paulin or Port Salut—creamy, buttery-rich and sweet with a light tangy aftertaste. The cheese is often marketed in a yellow plastic case.

Wines: Light whites and reds, nothing too fruity.
Serve: End of meals or as a snack.
Fat content: 50 per cent.
Type: Monastery.
Aroma: Unpronounced.

BONDON

A version of the French soft bloomy rind cheese Neufchâtel. Cheeses of this type have been produced in Normandy for centuries. (See *Neufchâtel*.)

BOULETTE D'AVESNES

Country of origin: France.

Background: This cheese is related to Maroilles. It was formerly a French farm cheese but is now being made by a number of commercial producers.

Description: The cheese is produced in the shape of a small cone, no more than 7.5 cm (3 in) in diameter and 10 cm (4 in) high. It has a natural red-tinted rind and a soft greyish interior. Made from cow's milk, Boulette d'Avesnes is produced by taking flawed Maroilles, mashing them and adding herbs such as parsley, tarragon and pepper. It is then ripened in damp cellars for three months.

To the uninitiated, d'Avesnes has an arresting flavour, to say the least—somewhat reminiscent of an over-ripe continental sausage. Its aroma matches its taste—extremely sharp and pronounced in both smell and flavour—not a cheese for the faint-hearted.

Boulette de Cambrai is a variation made in the shape of a small ball. This cheese does not undergo the three-month ripening period and is pure white in colour with less aroma and strength of flavour than d'Avesnes. Similar herbs are used to flavour it.

Boulette de la Pierre-Qui-Vire is another fresh, unripened variation of this cheese, more aromatic than de Cambrai.

Wines: Full-bodied reds.
Serve: End of meals; snacks.
Fat content: 50 per cent.
Type: Strong smelling/monastery.
Aroma: Pronounced.

BOURSAULT

Country of origin: France.

Background: This is a popular and widely marketed variety of one of the many types of French triple crème cheeses.

Description: Boursault is made in the shape of a small cylinder about 7.5 cm (3 in) in diameter and 5 cm (2 in) thick. Like all triple crèmes it is made from cow's milk enriched with cream. It is creamy off-white in colour and has a very thin, bloomy rind, soft and downy. The more down you see on the outside of the cheese, the older and stronger it is likely to be. Boursault is a very rich tasting cheese, lush, soft and creamy.

Wines: Any dessert wine, traminers, sauternes; alternatively fruity reds.
Serve: With fresh fruit—particularly apples, strawberries or pears; alternatively, sprinkle with pepper and serve with plain cracker biscuits; good with coffee.
Fat content: 75 per cent.
Type: Triple crème.
Aroma: Unpronounced.

BOURSIN

Country of origin: France.

Background: One of the new French triple crème cheeses which have become extremely popular in recent years.

Description: Due to its high cream content, Boursin is not for the diet-conscious. The cheese is often made in the shape of a small cylinder 7.5 cm (3 in) in diameter and 5 cm (2 in) high. It has a high per cent fat content which gives it a buttery texture and exceptional softness.

Boursin can be eaten in its natural state, when it is pure white in colour. French manufacturers, however, have produced several variations by adding aromatic herbs such as rosemary, fennel, chives and garlic. There is also a variety covered with pepper. The cheese itself is mild and rich, like all double and triple crème cheeses. When flavoured with herbs the predominant taste sensation is that of the herb, offset by the rich creaminess of the cheese itself.

Wines: Serve the plain variety with light dry whites, reds and rosés; the fine herb varieties with white burgundy, burgundy; the pepper variety with cabernet sauvignon or vintage port.
Serve: End of meals or as a luxurious and totally self-indulgent snack—with thin biscuits or wafers of crisp apple.
Fat content: 70-75 per cent.
Type: Triple crème.
Aroma: Unpronounced.

BRAIDED CHEESE

This is an Armenian cheese which has become quite popular in the USA. 'Ropes' of the cheese are braided (the ropes are just under 2.5 cm (1 in) in diameter and packaged in 250 g (8 oz) and 500 g (1 lb) packages. The cheese has caraway seeds lightly dispersed through it. Because of its pronounced salty flavour, it is first soaked in water; the cheese can then be pulled apart in strings and eaten as an appetiser.
(See Spiced Cheeses.)

BRESCIANO

An Italian Grana cheese used for grating.
(See Grana and Parmesan.)

BRESSAN

This is a French goat's milk cheese (*chèvre*) which is made in the shape of a truncated cone. (It is sometimes made with half goat's milk, half cow's milk.) Its fat content ranges from 40 to 45 per cent and the cheese measures only 4 cm (1½ in) in diameter and is about the same in height. Weight is 60 g (2 oz). This is not one of the milder tasting French chèvres. Bressan has a noticeably 'goaty' aroma and taste; older cheeses are very full and pronounced in flavour.
(See *Chèvres*.)

BRICK

Country of origin: USA.

Background: Most American cheeses are derived from Europe, but Brick is one of the few native originals. It was first made in the 1870s in Wisconsin which is still the principal state of its manufacture. It takes its name from its shape and also the probability that in its early days, bricks were used to mould it.

Description: This semi-soft cheese is rectangular shaped, measuring 25 cm (10 in) long, 12.5 cm (5 in) wide and 7.5 cm (3 in) deep. Brick is a surface-moulded cheese, with a reddish-brown rind which can be waxed. Its interior is a white-yellow scattered with small irregular shaped holes.

The cheese, made from cow's milk, undergoes a ripening period of up to three months at a temperature containing a high degree of humidity. It is washed quite regularly with salt water.

In texture and taste, Brick could be described as something of a half-way house between Cheddar and Limburger. The body of the cheese is firmer than Limburger but softer than Cheddar. It is mild, sweetish tasting but with a certain pungency, tangy and tasty. Brick also has a distinctive aroma, but nowhere near as overpowering as a well-ripened Limburger. Brick's texture is supple and the cheese slices well.

Wines: Fruity reds.
Serve: Widely used as a buffet and sandwich cheese; Brick melts easily and is well suited for grilling on bread.
Fat content: 50 per cent.
Type: Monastery, washed rind style.
Aroma: Distinctive.

BRIE

Country of origin: France.

Background: Brie is another cheese staking a claim as the 'king' of cheeses, although it is sometimes referred to as the 'queen'. It was actually given the title of 'king of cheeses' in 1815 at the Congress of Vienna which met at the end of the Napoleonic Wars for the more serious task of reorganising the states of Europe. At one of the various ceremonial dinners that took place during the Congress, a competition to choose the best cheese in the world was held. The veteran French statesman Talleyrand produced a Brie de Meaux—which won hands down. Many experts still feel that it has yet to be toppled from its throne.

Description: There is no doubt that a good Brie is an absolutely delicious cheese, surpassing Camembert, in many people's opinion, for delicacy of taste.

Like Camembert, Brie is a surface-ripened cheese made from cow's milk, which develops a 'flowery' outer crust through the activity of bacterial micro-organisms. The crust is downy white, usually scattered with patches of reddish brown pigments. The soft interior paste is rich yellow. The cheese is usually ripened for between three and four weeks.

Brie is a flat, disc-shaped cheese which is made in sizes ranging from 32.5 cm (13 in) to 40 cm (16 in) in diameter. It can be as little as 2.5 cm (1 in) thick.

Brie has a creamy, honey-like flavour with a hint of mushrooms, very rich, ripe and fruity, both subtle and tangy at the same time. Getting the cheese at its peak of condition is half the battle. When cut (most Brie is sold in wedges cut from the main cheese) it is easy to tell when it is at its best, for the straw-yellow interior paste is loose, flowing and bulg-

ing out of the confines of its outer crust. The crust, incidentally, is quite edible. Once the cheese has been cut it should be eaten on the day of purchase or very shortly thereafter as it will not keep.

Avoid a cheese that shows an excessive amount of reddish pigmentation on its crust or one that smells of ammonia—it is likely to be over-ripe. Brie does have a light smell of mould but the smell should never be overpronounced or penetrating—this is another sign of an over-aged cheese. If the cheese is under-ripe it will probably have a chalk-coloured, quite hard section in the centre.

Your best and simplest guide to quality when buying a cut wedge of Brie is to check the consistency of texture and colour of the interior paste. This paste should be the same throughout the cheese from top to bottom—a gold yellow in colour, soft, rich and glossy looking.

Wines: Fruity red wines.
Serve: End of meals; with a tossed salad for lunch. An aged Brie will dry out and shrivel but need not be discarded. Dipped in raw egg, coated with breadcrumbs, pan-fried and served with blackberry jam, it will make a delicious and unusual dessert.
Fat content: Minimum 45 per cent.
Type: Brie/Camembert family.
Aroma: Unpronounced.

Some of the Bries sold on the world market include:

AMERICAN BRIE: This is a good copy, rich and creamy but milder and not as strong and full-flavoured as the French.

AUSTRALIAN BRIE: This cheese has a harder, darker crust and a thicker, almost treacle-like texture. The cheese runs very freely, has the right creaminess in its flavour and also the distinct flavour of mushrooms.

BRIE DE MEAUX (France): The classic Brie rated by many experts as the best Brie in France. (Many cheese experts, incidentally, don't rate Bries made outside of France as worthy of serious consideration.) Brie de Meaux is made in large flat disc shapes up to

35 cm (14 in) in diameter, 2.5 cm (1 in) thick. In flavour and quality it has all the looked-for characteristics: rich, full, fruity and tangy but creamily soft and delicate at the same time, with a honey-like consistency to its golden interior paste. Brie de Meaux *fermier* is the farm produced variety; you'll be lucky to come by it but if you do you'll have a chance to sample one of the great delights of the cheese world.

BRIE DE MELUN (France): One of the oldest of the French Bries and highly regarded. Rather more pronounced in taste than Meaux and darker in colour, but still possessing the characteristic delicate richness and creaminess of taste.

COULOMMIERS (France): This is basically a smaller version of Brie de Meaux. It is a younger, fresher cheese which often does not acquire the reddish brown pigmentation on its crust.

DANISH BRIE: A good Danish cheese, with a slightly more rubbery texture than the French varieties. It is creamy and rich but slightly sharper tasting; it is not as sweet as the French styles and does not run.

GERMAN BRIE: Creamy yellow in colour, aromatic, with a slightly sour, mildly piquant taste.

SAISOF (France): Similar to Melun but somewhat milder and less rich and creamy.

BRIE DE COULOMMIERS

(See *Coulommiers.*)

BRILLAT-SAVARIN

A French triple crème, made in a disc shape about 12.5 cm (5 in) in diameter and some 5 cm (2 in) thick. This is another cheese from Normandy. It has a 75 per cent fat content

and is very rich, luscious and creamy with a very light sourish tinge.
(See *Triple Crèmes*.)

BRINZA

Country of origin: Hungary.

Background: This is 'pickled' cheese—that is, it is matured in brine for a period. It is made in several Balkan countries, being related to Feta. Versions of Brinza are also produced in America.

Description: Brinza, which is made from sheep's milk, is matured for four weeks. The cheese has no rind, a semi-soft texture and comes in a great variety of shapes, sizes and weights, most often appearing in the form of a solid, near-white, rather moist mass. In common with all cheeses that are matured in brine, Brinza has a distinctively salty taste, being quite sharp but also creamy in flavour. The cheese can also be made from goat's milk.

Wines: Full bodied reds; beer.
Serve: As a snack on bread or with tangy vegetables such as onions and radishes.
Fat content: 45 per cent.
Type: Sheep's milk.
Aroma: Noticeable sheep's milk smell.

BRIOLER

A German cheese made in 10 cm (4 in) square shapes which is similar to Limburger.
(See *Limburger*.)

BRIQUETTE

This is one of the many versions of the French cheese Neufchâtel produced in Normandy. Although they appear under many names and in many shapes they are all basically the same cheese—a small, soft, bloomy rind cream cheese. Neufchâtel is by far the best known.
(See *Neufchâtel*.)

BROCOTTE

A whey, Cottage style cheese, the best known version of which is Ricotta.
(See *Ricotta*.)

BROD

This was the name by which the Danish cheese Elbo was once known. It means 'bread cheese'.
(See *Elbo*.)

BUCHERON

A French goat's milk cheese or *chèvre*. This one is larger than most and is made in a log shape. It has a snow white, chalky texture and a mild but subtle goat cheese flavour.
(See *Chèvres*.)

BUKO

Brand name for a Danish processed cheese spread range.
(See *Processed Cheese*.)

BURRINO

Country of origin: Italy.

Background: This cheese is also known as Manteca, Manteche, Butirro, Burriello, and Burro. Its most unusual feature is that it has a knob of butter in the centre of the cheese curd. *Burro* is the Italian word for butter.

Description: The cheese is made in a gourd shape, in the same fashion as Provolone. The cheese is about 10 cm (4 in) in height and because it is smoked it is a yellow-brown in colour. The knob of butter inside the cheese is yellow. When cut down the middle, the difference in texture and colour of butter and curd makes an appealing combination. The cheese is mild tasting with an obviously buttery flavour.

Wines: Light reds, dry whites.
Serve: Snacks; an unusual cheese to serve at end of meals sprinkled with black pepper.
Fat content: 45 per cent.
Type: Bland/buttery.
Aroma: Unpronounced.

BUTTER CHEESE

Country of origin: Germany.

Background: This cheese is also known as Damenkäse or 'ladies cheese'. It is a very mild and bland cheese in marked contrast to the German sour curd and skimmed milk varieties.

Description: An extremely undemanding cheese, soft, rich, creamy and bland. It is made in sausage shapes or in the form of small loaves and has a brown to pale red outer skin. Its interior is smooth, free of holes and with the consistency and colour of butter. The cheese is virtually odourless and mild with just a slightly sour quality to its taste.

The Germans put this into the category of semi-soft, sliceable cheeses.

Wines: Light red wines, rosés, light whites.
Serve: End of meals, snacks.
Fat content: 50 per cent.
Type: Bland/buttery.
Aroma: Unpronounced.

CABOC

A double crème Scottish cheese which is rolled in oatmeal. The cheese is made in small log shapes about 10 cm (4 in) in length and weighs approximately 120 g (4 oz).
(See *Double Crèmes*.)

CABRION

A French goat's milk cheese from Burgundy soaked in marc and ripened in fresh husks of newly-pressed grapes.
(See *Chèvres*.)

CACIOCAVALLO

Country of origin: Italy.

Background: This cheese, which comes from the region of Naples, dates back to the Middle Ages. Many theories have been advanced for the origin of its name, which means 'horse cheese'.

One explanation has it that the cheese was once made from mare's milk; another that it was simply named after Monte Cavallo in Italy where it was first made. At one time the cheese was imprinted with a galloping horse—the mark of the kingdom of Naples. *Larousse Gastronomique* states that the name comes from the ripening process, when the cheeses are straddled in pairs over sticks—like packs on a horse.

Caciocavallo is a *pasta filata* variety, so called because the curd is immersed in hot water, and worked into shape by hand while it is easily malleable. As the cheese curd is cut into small pieces during the making process or 'cheddared', Caciocavallo is related to the Cheddar family of cheeses.

Description: Caciocavallo is moulded by hand into a gourd-like shape with a narrow end or 'neck' which allows the cheeses to be roped together in pairs and left to ripen. The cheese, made from cow's milk, measures some 12.5 cm (5 in) in diameter and 40 cm (16 in) in length.

Caciocavallo is dark yellow in colour with an ivory white interior and a firm, smooth-textured body when young.

Young cheeses, which are ripened for about four months, are mild but with a tang tasting rather like a young Cheddar; aged for twelve months or more they acquire a pronounced spicy and salty sharpness and a hard, granular texture. They are then used for grating and cooking. This cheese is a forebear of the popular Italian cooking cheese Provolone. Unlike Provolone, Caciocavallo is not always smoked and has a slightly lower fat content.

Wines: Light fruity reds for young cheeses; heavy red wines for older cheeses.
Serve: Young cheeses can be served at the table with bread, biscuits and fruits such as pineapple, dried apricots and red and green

peppers; aged Caciocavallo is used for grating.
Fat content: 44 per cent.
Type: Extra hard grating cheese/Cheddar.
Aroma: Unpronounced.

CACIOTTA

This is the name given to a large range of Italian country cheeses which are made from cow's, goat's or sheep's milk. They are all simple, unsophisticated rural cheeses usually produced in small sizes and given individual names related to where they are made. Two of the best known are Cacio Fiore and Cacio Fiore Aquilano. They are similar to the stracchino style cheeses—soft, white, mild and delicate tasting. Unlikely to be seen outside Italy. (See *Stracchino*.)

CAERPHILLY

Country of origin: Great Britain (Wales).

Background: This is one of the nine famous 'champion' cheeses—the traditional English cheeses. It takes its name from Caerphilly, a small town seven miles north of Cardiff. The cheese, which has been eaten there for centuries, has always been a great favourite with the Welsh miners, who would take it with them to the coalface for a lunchtime snack. The miners appreciated Caerphilly's salty tang when working underground, perhaps because its salt content replaced the salt lost through excessive perspiration in the hot and humid conditions of the mines. The miners found, too, that the cheese remained fresh and moist under these conditions.

Description: Caerphilly is a white, mild cheese that takes only two weeks to mature. It is semi-soft, rather flaky in texture with a definite salty flavour. Its mildness makes it easily digestible and the cheese leaves a clean, fresh taste on the palate. Caerphilly has been aptly described as a 'gentle' cheese.

Like the other eight 'champion' cheeses of England, Caerphilly is made in cylindrical shapes weighing up to 4.5 kg (10 lb); in rindless blocks weighing up to 20 kg (45 lb) and is

also sold in small vacuum-packed pieces. As with all cheeses, its flavour sharpens with age; Caerphilly bought outside the UK will not be as fresh and will taste altogether less delicate. Its salty tang will be more pronounced and it will develop a noticeable 'bite'.

Wines: Dry madeira, fairly dry sherry, hock or a dry rosé.
Serve: End of meals; as a snack with celery and thin slices of bread and butter.
Fat content: 45 per cent.
Type: Cheddar family.
Aroma: Unpronounced.

CALCAGNO

A Pecorino style hard, grating cheese from Sicily.
(See *Pecorino Romano*.)

CAMEMBERT

Country of origin: France.

Background: One of the world's most famous cheeses—again one created by the French. Camembert comes from Normandy which, as early as the twelfth century, had a reputation as a cheesemaking centre.

A Madame Marie Harel, a farmer's wife, is said to have created Camembert around 1790, although it is more likely that the good lady brought to a final stage of development what was a traditional-style cheese of the area. Whatever the truth of the matter, the cheese became a favourite of Napoleon's and the French put up statues in her honour.

Camembert started on the road to worldwide fame in 1890 when it was first packaged in small cylindrical boxes. Before this, the cheese was traditionally wrapped in straw, which meant that it could not travel long distances without becoming spoiled.

Description: The art of eating Camembert is to get it at what the experts call *à point*—that is, at the optimum peak of ripeness. Take advice from your cheese seller on this, but there are certain checks you can make your-

self. A Camembert in good condition has a slightly off-white 'mouldy' crust covered with fine down and lightly touched with reddish pigmentation. (Camemberts made outside France tend to be whiter.) The interior paste is creamy yellow with a honey-like fluidity that is the same consistency throughout. When the cheese is cut and it is at its peak, this paste will bulge out from beneath its crust in one solid soft mass. The average sized cheese is approximately 11 cm (4½ in) in diameter and 3.75 cm (1½ in) thick.

A ripe Camembert should be supple and will feel tender and springy when squeezed gently across its diameter. The cheese should never be hard, shrunken or excessively pigmented with red mould or smell of ammonia. All these things are signs of an over-aged, over-ripe cheese. An under-ripe cheese will not have the necessary fluid consistency in its interior and may have a hardish chalky mid-section.

Camembert is a cheese that ripens from the outside—that is, it is surface ripened. It develops its 'mouldy' crust as a result of being treated with a *Penicillium* spore. The crust, known as a 'flowery' or 'bloomy' rind because of the delicate mould that grows on its surface, is quite edible, but not when it is dried out and shrunken.

The cheese, which is made from cow's milk, is produced in small flat disc shapes and spends between one and two months ripening before marketing. Camembert has no pronounced aroma, apart from a light, fresh and not unpleasant smell of mould. There are so many different makes of Camembert that its flavour varies considerably. At its best it is delicately mild but with a rich, delicious and creamy tang. Camembert is a cheese which should be eaten at its peak, within a day or so of purchase —it will not keep and quickly passes its prime.

The cheese is produced in countries all over Europe and in countries as far apart as Australia and the USA, but the French varieties, of which there are many, are generally acknowledged as the finest.

Similar style cheeses include Brie, Carré de l'Est and Chaource.

Wines: Claret; light dry whites.
Serve: End of meals; a Camembert served with fresh tomatoes, capsicum, rye bread and a lightly tossed salad makes a delectable lunch; an over-aged Camembert can be coated with raw egg, dipped in breadcrumbs, pan-fried and then served with jam for an arresting and offbeat dessert.
Fat content: 45-50 per cent.
Type: Brie/Camembert family.
Aroma: Unpronounced.

CANESTRATO

Also known as Pecorino Siciliano, this is a sheep's milk cheese which is the Sicilian version of Pecorino Romano. A *canestro* is the draining basket used during the making process; the marks of the basket can be seen on the cheese. A good, fulsome, rustic table cheese; aged versions are used for grating.
(See *Pecorino Romano*.)

CANTAL

Country of origin: France.

Background: One of the oldest of the French cheeses which is believed to date back to Roman days. Cantal is made on the slopes of the Auvergne mountains and is a member of the Cheddar family.

Description: Cantal is a hard, yellow cheese made from cow's milk in cylindrical shapes up to 40 cm (16 in) high and 45 cm (18 in) in diameter. It has a cloth-covered, greyish rind beneath which is a light yellow interior paste, free of holes but sometimes with a few cracks. The interior texture is firm, resilient and supple. Large Cantals can weigh as much as 54 kg (120 lb) but smaller sized cheeses which weigh in the region of 7 kg (16 lb) are made. The cheese, which undergoes a 'cheddaring' process, is ripened for periods varying between three and six months.

In taste, the cheese is similar to a good mature Cheddar, mellow, fulsome but with a rather sweetish, nutty flavour. Older Cantals develop a greater pungency and bite.

Wines: Fruity beaujolais-style reds; also goes with beer.
Serve: A first class all-purpose table cheese.

Fat content: 45 per cent.
Type: Cheddar.
Aroma: Rich milky aroma when cut.

CAPRICE DES DIEUX

Country of origin: France.

Background: A double crème cheese from the Champagne area.

Description: Caprice des Dieux is a Brie/Camembert style double crème cheese. It is matured for several weeks so that it develops the typical bloomy rind of cheeses of this type, pure white flecked with pink-brown pigmentation. The interior paste is cream white, soft, spreadable, rich and buttery. The cheese takes the shape of an oval loaf about 14 cm (5½ in) long, is under 5 cm (2 in) high and weighs around 250 g (8 oz). It is marketed in a cardboard box.

In flavour the cheese, with its high fat content, is like a richer Brie or Camembert, uncomplicated but thick and luscious.

Wines: Fruity reds but also goes with full flavoured whites.
Serve: End of meals with fresh fruit; essentially a dessert cheese.
Fat content: 60 per cent.
Type: Double crème, Brie/Camembert style.
Aroma: Unpronounced.
(See *Double Crèmes*.)

CAPRICETTE

This is a French skimmed goat's milk cheese with a delicate texture and soft, creamy flavour. It is marketed in 90 g (3 oz) plastic cups. A good mild cheese to start with if you're interested in acquiring a taste for goat's milk cheeses.
(See *Chèvres*.)

CAPRINO

Generic term for a range of semi-soft goat's milk cheeses from the Argentine.

CAPRINO ROMANO

The goat's milk version of the Italian grating cheese Pecorino Romano which is made from sheep's milk.
(See *Pecorino Romano*.)

CARRE DE L'EST

Country of origin: France.

Background: This cheese comes from Alsace-Lorraine. Its name means square cheese of the east.

Description: This is a soft, bloomy-rind cheese similar to Camembert. It differs from Camembert in its shape, being made in 10 cm (4 in) squares about 2.5 cm (1 in) thick. The cheese, which is ripened for a three week period, has the familiar downy white or bloomy rind of a Camembert and the creamy ivory-white interior paste. It has a slight mushroomy aroma.

Carré de l'Est is made from cow's milk. In flavour it is reminiscent of Camembert but rather blander and less sophisticated; it can be looked on as an interesting but simpler and milder version of the more famous Normandy cheese. American-made Camemberts are considered to be somewhat similar in taste to Carré de l'Est.

Wines: Light reds and dry whites.
Serve: End of meals; lunch-time snacks.
Fat content: 45-50 per cent.
Type: Camembert/Brie.
Aroma: Unpronounced.
(See *Camembert*.)

CASIGIOLU

A member of the Italian pasta filata (drawn curd) family of cheeses. The best known cheeses of this type are Provolone and Caciocavallo, widely used in cooking for a variety of Italian style dishes.
(See *Pasta Filata* and *Provolone*.)

CENDRES

The name given to a range of French cheeses that are ripened in ashes. They are usually produced in the wine growing areas of France and are unlikely to be seen outside their country of origin.

CHABICHOU

Country of origin: France.

Background: A well rated French *chèvre* from the Poitou province of France produced both commercially and on farms. It is sometimes known as Cabichou, Cabrichiu or Chabi.

Description: Chabichou is a soft, natural rind goat's milk cheese made in a truncated cone shape about 7 cm (2½ in) across and 5 cm (2 in) high. Some are made in rectangle shapes. The farm-produced Chabichous, known as Chabis, have a bluish rind, the factory-made ones a white rind. The cheeses are ripened in dry cellars for about three weeks. They weigh about 90 g (3 oz).

In flavour, Chabichous are decidedly 'goaty', quite pronounced, fruity and intense; farmhouse varieties are usually stronger flavoured than commercially produced ones. Either way, a cheese for those who like a strong flavour; the aroma is equally noticeable.

Wines: Nothing fancy, an inexpensive, fruity red.
Serve: End of meals.
Fat content: 45 per cent.
Type: Goat's milk.
Aroma: Pronouncedly 'goaty'.
(See *Chèvres*.)

CHAOURCE

Another French Camembert style cheese measuring 10 cm (4 in) in diameter and 6 cm (2½ in) high. The cheese has a soft downy white and a rich pale yellow interior. A soft, rich cheese with a mild but fruity taste with a hint of mushrooms in the aroma. The cheese comes from the Champagne area and has a 45-50 per cent fat content.
(See *Camembert*.)

CHAUMES

A French variety of Limburger made in 25 cm (10 in) diameter wheel shapes 2.5 cm (1 in) thick. It has the orange coloured rind familiar to many other cheeses of this type.
(See *Limburger*.)

CHAVIGNOL

A French chèvre, or goat's milk cheese, also known as Crottin de Chavignol. Aged versions of this cheese can be quite overpowering in taste and aroma.
(See *Crottin de Chavignol* and *Chèvres*.)

CHEDDAR

Country of origin: Great Britain (England).

Background: Cheddar, the most popular and widely copied English cheese in the world, originally came from the Cheddar Gorge area in Somerset, where it has been made since the fifteenth century. The cheese gained widespread popularity in Tudor times and formerly was noted for the huge sizes in which it was made. Cheddars weighing 56 kg (126 lb) were commonplace and one made for Queen Victoria's wedding celebrations measured 3 m (9 ft) across. Giant Cheddars are now a thing of the past and fewer are made in the traditional cylindrical shape.

Description: Cheddar is now made all over the world, as far away as America and Australia. Cheddars vary considerably in taste, but the traditional English cheese is rich and nutty tasting with a close, creamy texture. The English put the cheese into two categories: mild, aged up to five months, with a characteristic clean and mellow but not pronounced flavour; and mature, aged eight months or more, a

cheese with the same background but with a pronounced and more full-blooded bite.

The colour of Cheddar ranges from near white for the younger varieties to a richer amber yellow for the mature cheeses. (A Cheddar's colouring is sometimes achieved by the use of annatto, a vegetable dye—but this is not always the case.) English Cheddar is made in large cylindrical shapes and in rindless blocks weighing about 4.5 kg (10 lb) and 20 kg (45 lb); it is also sold in small vacuum-packed pieces.

The name Cheddar comes from the village in Somerset where the cheese originated, but it also refers to a step in the manufacturing process known as 'cheddaring'. Very simply, this means that at the stage when sufficient whey has been drained from the cheese, the curd is allowed to matt and is cut into 15 cm (6 in) blocks. These blocks are 'cheddared' by being continually turned and stacked on the bottom of the cheese vat at intervals of 10-15 minutes for about $1\frac{1}{2}$ hours.

The majority of English Cheddar is factory produced but the best, and the hardest to come by, is that made on farms. These are known as Farmhouse Cheddars and were traditionally made from unpasteurised milk. Pasteurised Farmhouse Cheddars are also available and are sold on the world market.

Wines: The choice varies as widely as the cheese: use full-bodied wines for mature Cheddars, lighter wines for the milder, younger cheeses; beer goes with all varieties.
Serve: Cheddar is one of the best all-purpose table cheeses in the world; it can be used in salads, in sauces, in omelettes, with fruit, for toasted bread snacks or even with ham and crisp bacon.
Fat content: 45 per cent.
Type: Cheddar.
Aroma: Unpronounced.

Other Cheddars sold around the world include:

AMERICAN CHEDDAR: English settlers brought the recipe for Cheddar to America and today numerous cheeses of this type are produced. The first American cheese factory, established in 1851 in Oneida County, New York, was devoted to the production of Cheddar cheese. Today, it is estimated that nearly 70 per cent of the cheese produced in the United States is Cheddar, the largest part of it coming from Wisconsin.

American Cheddars run the full gamut of mild to strong tasting cheeses, differing greatly in taste, texture, firmness and hardness of body. Varieties include:

Coon: A highly regarded cheese from New York State, noted for its sharp pronounced taste. This is achieved by ripening in an atmosphere with a high temperature and a high degree of humidity—higher, that is, than is normal for Cheddar. The cheese has a dark chocolate-coloured rind and a very pale interior and is one of the most full-flavoured of American Cheddars.

Gold'n Rich: A semi-soft Cheddar with a cult following of its own, particularly in mid-west America.

Kaukauna Klub: A popular Cheddar-style cheese sold in china crocks. This type of cheese is known as coldpack cheese. It is made by blending two cheeses together as with processed cheese. Unlike processed cheese it is not subject to heating. Coldpack cheese is quite soft, spreadable and has good keeping qualities.

Monterey: This cheese comes from California and is also known as Monterey Jack or simply Jack. It comes in two varieties, one made from whole cow's milk and ripened for up to six weeks and one made from skimmed milk and matured for some six months. The young Monterey is quite soft and delicate tasting for a Cheddar; the older variety is sharper tasting, quite hard and is used as a grating cheese.

Pineapple: A cheese created in the early 1800s in Litchfield, Connecticut. While ripening, the cheese was hung in meshed nets which created corrugations on its surface similar to those on a pineapple. Last century the cheese was served on a platter with a silver top designed like pineapple leaves. This ensemble became a standard feature in middle class homes throughout the country—an early example of successful American marketing methods. Today the cheese is still made in the traditional pineapple shape and in a variety of sizes, the largest weighing around 3 kg ($6\frac{3}{4}$ lb).

English Farmhouse Cheddar

Vermont Cheddar: Rated amongst the best of American Cheddars, white, sharp—considered by some to be on a par with the highly-prized Canadian Cheddars.

Vermont Sage: A descendant of the English Derby Sage. The cheese was originally flavoured with fresh sage, but nowadays a sage extract is used which gives it a greenish hue and mottling. In taste it is like a mild Cheddar with a delicate sage flavouring—unusual and quite palatable.

Other well-known American Cheddars are Texas Longhorn, Young American, Daisy, Redskin, Tillamook, Twin Flats, Black Wax and Colorado Blackie.

AUSTRALIAN CHEDDAR: Cheddar is Australia's most popular cheese type, despite the development in recent years of a whole range of Continental-style cheeses. Australia classes her Cheddars as *mild* (matured for about three months), *semi-mature* (aged for three to six months), *mature* (aged for six months to one year), and *vintage* (aged 18 months).

In Queensland the areas of manufacture include the southern region, Woodford, Caboolture and Warwick; the west includes Toowoomba, situated on the edge of the Great Dividing Range, Mount Tyson and as far north as Millaa Millaa. In New South Wales the north coast and the Hunter River areas boast excellent Cheddars whilst the south coast is renowned with brands such as Bodalla, Kameruka, MacRobertson, Tilba Tilba.

In Victoria, Cheddars are found in the Gippsland and north-east regions of the state, extending to the Western District on the way to the south-east of South Australia where the famous Mount Gambier Cheddars exist. Western Australia, particularly in the south-west region at Coolup, Albany and the Margaret River manufacture excellent Cheddars which rarely travel to the eastern states.

Interesting varieties include Cheddar spiced with garlic and cumin. One Queensland variety, which is smoky flavoured, is studded with pieces of bacon; another is flavoured with peanuts.

Australia's processed Cheddar range includes cheeses spiced with flavourings as varied as garlic, spring onions and curry. Smoked processed Cheddar is also produced.

CANADIAN CHEDDAR: These cheeses enjoy an excellent reputation amongst Cheddar enthusiasts. They are made from unpasteurised cow's milk and many experts feel they are the only Cheddars that come near to the quality of a good English Farmhouse Cheddar. Two of the most highly acclaimed are known as Black Diamond and Cherry Hill. Because of health regulations unpasteurised Canadian Cheddars are not allowed to be exported to most countries; none for example, are shipped across the border to the USA.

NEW ZEALAND CHEDDAR: A wide range of good Cheddars is available marketed under names such as Anchor Mainland, Epicure, Anchor, Okato Matured. There is also a New Zealand Cheddar with port wine.

CHEEDAM

Country of origin: Australia.

Background: This is an Australian cheese that is a cross between Cheddar and Edam.

Description: Cheedam is a pale yellow in colour and comes in rectangular vacuum packed blocks approximately 15 cm (6 in) by 10 cm (4 in) by 5 cm (2 in). The Cheddar in its make-up is mild, as is the cheese— very bland, clean, faintly creamy tasting.

Wines: Any light red or dry white; beer.
Serve: An undemanding snack-type cheese.
Fat content: 45 per cent.
Type: Bland/buttery/Cheddar.
Aroma: Unpronounced.

CHERRY HILL

A very well regarded Canadian Cheddar which has the distinction of being made from unpasteurised cow's milk. Experts rate this cheese on a par with the very best English Farmhouse Cheddars.
(See Canadian *Cheddars*.)

CHESHIRE

Country of origin: Great Britain (England).

Background: Cheshire is considered the oldest of all the English cheeses. No one knows exactly how old it is, but it was certainly known in the county from which it takes its name in the twelfth century.

Description: There are three kinds of Cheshire —red, white and blue. All three have a slight tang to them, derived from the deposits of salt in the Cheshire soil. Carrot juice was supposed to have been used originally to give Red Cheshire its colouring, but nowadays an annatto dye has replaced it. Both the red and the white are loose, crumbly cheeses, the white being somewhat milder than the red.

The Blue Cheshire is the top of the batch— the richest and the rarest. This is all the more remarkable because Blue Cheshires come about by accident—that is, they develop the *Penicillium glaucum* spore naturally instead of having it injected into them as is done with other blue-veined cheeses. The Blue Cheshire is a rich, creamy blue-veined cheese which takes six months to mature. Today an increasing number of Blue Cheshires are produced by inoculating them with the *Penicillium* mould.

Wines: Red and White Cheshire with a light red or dry white wine; serve the Blue with port.
Serve: Like Cheddar, the Red and White Cheshires are stable all-purpose table cheeses that can be eaten at the end of a meal or served as snacks on bread or in sandwiches. They can also be used in the traditional Ploughman's Lunch—Cheshire, fresh crusty bread, butter, pickles, celery, tomato and a glass of beer. Serve the Blue at end of meals.
Fat content: 45 per cent.
Type: Cheddar.
Aroma: Unpronounced.

CHESTER

A French version of the traditional English Cheshire cheese. The cheese is made in tall cylinder shapes up to 45 cm (18 in) high. (See *Cheshire* and *Cheddar*.)

CHEVRES

Country of origin: France.

Description: Chèvres is the generic name for all French goat's milk cheeses. They are made in a great variety of shapes, which range from pyramids and balls to cones and small discs. Chèvres are usually made in small sizes, up to 250 g (8 oz). They vary in taste considerably —young cheeses are quite mild; older Chèvres can be ferociously pungent, rank and overpowering.

The rinds of some Chèvres are a bluish grey in colour, the result of the cheese being treated with wood ash; others have a light bloomy rind, off-white in colour, often patchily pigmented. Many Chèvres are still produced on farms, but most are factory produced by commercial producers. They all have a typical 'goatish' barnyardy flavour about them, although whether this is strongly pronounced depends on the age of the cheese. Some Chèvres have sheep's or cow's milk added to their goat's milk content.

Chèvres cheeses include Banon, Valençay, Crottin de Chavignol, Chabichou, Bucheron, Bressan, Pouligny-Saint-Pierre, Poivre d'Ane, Mothais and Sainte-Maure.

Chevrotin is a general name for a group of goat's milk cheeses from the Bourbonnais province of France. Such cheeses include Chevrotin du Bourbonnais, de Conne, des Moulins and de Souvigny.

Wines: Lively reds for a young cheese; more full-bodied red wines for the older cheeses.
Serve: End of meals; as a snack.
Fat content: Usually 45 per cent.
Type: Goat's milk cheeses.
Aroma: Young cheeses, unpronounced; older cheeses can be highly pronounced.

CHEVROTIN

Country of origin: France.

Background: Chevrotin is the name for a large range of French goat's milk cheeses which are made in the province of Bourbonnais, the best known one being Chevrotin du Bourbonnais.

English Cheshire (left), Australian Southbrook Cheshire (right)

Others include Chevrotin de Conne, Chevrotin de Moulins and Chevrotin de Souvigny.

Description: This range of cheeses is made in various shapes from small wheels measuring around 15 cm (6 in) in diameter to small 5 cm (2 in) high cones. Chevrotin is a semi-soft goat's milk cheese with a natural rind which is ripened for one or two weeks. It has a supple texture with a thin, lightly formed, bloomy rind. In flavour the cheese is quite rich tasting, creamy, nutty, full flavoured but not as 'goaty' as some other *chèvres*.

Wines: Light but fruity white wines.
Serve: End of meals.
Fat content: 45 per cent.
Type: Goat's milk.
Aroma: Not overpronounced but aged versions of this style of cheese will develop considerably in odour (and flavour).
(See *Chèvres*.)

CHILBERTA

Country of origin: France.

Background: This is probably the best known of a range of mountain cheeses made throughout the Pyrenees. Some are made from goat's milk, some cow's milk; Chilberta from the latter.

Description: Chilberta is a small, wheel shaped cheese about 5 cm (2 in) in height which weighs 250 g (8 oz). It has a thin orange-red rind and a semi-soft light yellow interior dotted with small, irregularly shaped holes. The cheese has a strong, earthy aroma reminiscent of many monastery-style cheeses; in flavour it is not over dramatic, but pleasantly tangy and tasty—a simple, agreeable, uncomplicated Basque country cheese.

Wines: Goes well with simple reds.
Serve: A good snack style cheese well suited to crusty French bread.
Fat content: 45 per cent.
Type: Monastery.
Aroma: Noticeable but not over-strong.

COEUR

One of the many versions of the French cheese Neufchâtel. This one is made in a heart shape but like Neufchâtel is essentially a small, soft, bloomy rind cream cheese.
(See *Neufchâtel*.)

COEUR A LA CREME

A variety of Fromage Blanc, a French fresh unripened cheese eaten with sugar and cream; it is moulded into a heart shape.
(See *Fromage Blanc*.)

COLBY

A soft textured American cheese rather similar to Cheddar but with a high moisture content and a rather sweetish flavour.
(See American *Cheddars*.)

COLDPACK CHEESE

This is not a processed cheese but is similar in that it is a combination of two cheeses, often Cheddars, which are mixed together. The difference is that Coldpack Cheese does not undergo a heating process. Coldpack Cheese is often sold in crocks; it is soft, more spreadable than natural cheeses and will keep longer. Kaukauna Klub is one example.

COLORADO BLACKIE

(See American *Cheddars*.)

COMMISSIE

A double-sized version of the Dutch cheese Edam. Commissie weighs between 3 and 4.5 kg (7-10 lb).
(See *Edam*.)

COMTE

Country of origin: France.

Background: This cheese, which dates back to the thirteenth century, is a French type of Gruyère. It is also known as Gruyère de Comté.

Description: The cheese has a hard, thick outer rind, a brownish yellow in colour, and a smooth, firm-textured pale yellow interior dotted with small holes the size of cherries. Comté is made in the shape of flattened cylindrical wheels up to 65 cm (26 in) in diameter and 10 cm (4 in) thick. It weighs in the region of 40 kg (90 lb).

Like Gruyère, Comté is a cooked, pressed cheese. It is similar in taste to the Swiss cheese, but less sweet, slightly sharper with rather more bite. Its flavour can become quite pronounced with age.

Wines: Light but full grape-flavoured dry whites and reds.
Serve: A good cheese for the cheeseboard at end of meals; it is also an excellent cooking cheese for such dishes as fondues.
Fat content: 45 per cent.
Type: Swiss.
Aroma: Unpronounced.

COON

A highly regarded and quite sharp and pronounced Cheddar from New York State. The cheese is ripened in an atmosphere with a high temperature and high humidity.
(See American *Cheddars*.)

CORNHUSKER

This is an American Cheddar similar to Colby, developed by the Nebraska Agricultural Experiment Station in 1940. It has a softer texture than Cheddar and contains more moisture, and therefore does not keep as long.
(See American *Cheddars*.)

COROLLE DU POITOU

Although from the Poitou region of France, well known for its goat's milk cheeses, this cheese is made from cow's milk. It is a double crème Camembert/Brie style cheese with a 60 per cent fat content. The cheese has a firm centre with creamy edges and a white downy surface.
(See *Double Crèmes*.)

COTHERSTONE

This is a rare Yorkshire cheese sometimes known as Yorkshire Stilton. A blue vein that resembles Stilton, it was first produced in the Tees Valley, Yorkshire, England. Highly considered but extremely hard to come by.

COTSWOLD

Country of origin: Great Britain (England).

Background: This is one of several new varieties of English cheese flavoured with various additives.

Description: Cotswold is a version of the traditional English cheese Double Gloucester with chives added. It has the smooth, mellow taste of the typical Gloucester with the chives imparting a fragrant, delicate, oniony flavour.

Wine: Light reds; also goes well with beer.
Serve: End of meals; lunch with a light salad and beer.
Fat content: 45 per cent.
Type: Cheddar family.
Aroma: Unpronounced.

COTTAGE CHEESE

Country of origin: Unknown.

Background: This fresh, unripened cheese, originally made from naturally soured milk, is one of the oldest forms of cheese known to

man. It was developed before the ripening process was discovered—possibly the accidental result of one of these cheeses being stored and forgotten.

Description: The cheese is simply made by milk being set with a lactic starter, cut, drained of whey and then packed. The cheese is not ripened. In appearance it takes the form of a lumpy white mass made up of small white curd particles.

There are many varieties of Cottage Cheese on the market which differ greatly in the way they are made, their fat content and their flavour. One of the most popular is the American and Australian bland-flavoured curd style, made from skimmed milk.

The curd of American and Australian Cottage Cheese receives repeated washings, which cuts down the acidity of the cheese and results in a flavour bland to very mildly acid. Cream is often added to give the cheese extra moisture and a more attractive flavour. The cheese is usually marketed in plastic containers. Creamed Cottage Cheese is available with flavourings as varied as gherkin and pineapple.

Continental-style Cottage Cheese is often marketed in cellophane or plastic envelopes or sausage-shaped packs. This cheese is not washed during its manufacture and its flavour is therefore sharper and more acid. There is little separation in the cheese and it appears as a solid packed mass. Its chief use lies in cooking.

Cottage Cheese is also known as Pot Cheese, Dutch Cheese and Schmierkäse. In America it is sometimes called Popcorn Cheese—in reference to its curd particles.

In all its forms Cottage Cheese has great appeal to dieters and weight watchers because of its low fat and calorie content.

Varieties can have a fat content of between 4 and 15 per cent, depending on the manufacturer. The Continental-style non-fat Cottage Cheese has up to only 4 per cent fat content.

Wines: Not really applicable, but a light rosé or white wine is a possibility.
Serve: The bland American Cottage Cheese goes with salad vegetables, on open sandwiches or as a base for potato salads or appetisers. Alternatively, it can be served on a dessert platter with fresh fruits such as strawberries,

peaches, melon, grapes or pineapple. The sharper flavour of Continental Cottage Cheese makes it less popular in salads and sweet dishes, but is often used in cheesecakes, savoury or dessert soufflés, fillings for pancakes, cannelloni or lasagne dishes or as a base for dips and spreads.
Fat content: Varies between 4-15 per cent.
Type: Fresh, unripened.
Aroma: Unpronounced.

COULOMMIERS

Country of origin: France.

Background: This cheese can be considered a small-sized version of Brie. It takes its name from the town in the Seine et Marne region where it is made.

Description: Coulommiers is a soft, disc-shaped cheese 12.5 cm (5 in) in diameter and 2.5 cm (1 in) thick, made from cow's milk. It is very similar in appearance to Brie, having a downy white, bloomy rind and a soft, creamy yellow, loosely flowing interior. The cheese has a pleasantly fresh bouquet and the delectable rich, creamy, fruity Brie-type flavour.

Coulommiers is ripened for a four-week period. As with all cheeses of this type, it will not keep and should be eaten soon after purchase. Larger versions of this cheese measuring 25 cm (10 in) in diameter are known as Brie de Coulommiers.

Wines: Light but fruity reds.
Serve: End of meals.
Fat content: 45-50 per cent.
Type: Camembert/Brie.
Aroma: Unpronounced.
(See *Brie*.)

CREAM CHEESE

Country of origin: Unknown.
Background: Like Cottage Cheese, this is one of the most ancient forms of cheese in the world. An English version known as Slipcote was extremely popular in Shakespeare's time. Mrs Beaton did not think it should be classed

as a cheese at all. She wrote: 'Cream cheese, although so-called, is not properly cheese, but is nothing more than cream dried sufficiently to be cut with a knife.'

Description: Cream Cheese is a soft, rich, fresh unripened cheese made in a similar fashion to Cottage Cheese. The main difference is that Cream Cheese is made from milk and cream, which is added after the whey has been drained from the milk-curd. This results in a soft, white, rindless smooth-textured mass of cheese with a rich and mildly acid flavour. The cheese is usually marketed foil-wrapped, in tubs or plastic containers.

The term 'cream cheese' is also used more generally in reference to double and triple crème cheeses (cheeses with an exceptionally high fat content) and soft, bloomy rind cheeses such as Neufchâtel. These are very different types of cream cheese and should not be confused with the cheese under discussion here.

Wines: A light rosé; alternatively coffee or tea.
Serve: Fresh Cream Cheese is used in cheese-cakes, gelatine-based desserts and savoury snacks. It can also be used in dips, served with dry biscuits, dried fruits, carrot and celery sticks, cucumber wedges, pretzels or pressed fruits. It is an excellent base for dessert and savoury cooking and can be delicious with seasonal fresh fruits as a whipped creamy topping.
Fat content: 35-38 per cent.
Type: Fresh, unripened.
Aroma: Unpronounced.

CREMA DANIA

Country of origin: Denmark.

Background: This cheese, which first appeared in the late 1950s, was the creation of one Henrik Tholstrup of Copenhagen. In many ways it is similar to Brie but has a much higher fat content.

Description: Crema Dania is made from cow's milk enriched with cream. The cheese is made in rectangular bar shapes weighing about 180 g (6 oz) and comes foil-wrapped in a cardboard box. The cheese has a thin bloomy white rind developed after a three-week ripening period, and a smooth, yellow-white interior. The interior paste is creamy and soft, very easy to spread. The cheese ripens very evenly and when at its best has a rich gloss. In taste, the cheese is Brie-like, very rich, creamy, smooth and delectable. It is considered one of Denmark's most notable contributions to the cheese world. Crema Dania's high fat content makes it a double crème cheese, almost a triple crème.

A similar cheese, also Danish, is Crème Royale.

Wines: Light reds; dry whites; light rosés.
Serve: Serve as a dessert with fruits such as strawberries.
Fat content: 72 per cent.
Type: Double crème.
Aroma: Unpronounced.

CREME CHERRY

Brand name for a Norwegian processed cheese range.
(See *Processed Cheese*.)

CREME DE GRUYERE

A French range of processed cheese.
(See *Processed Cheese*.)

CREME DE SAVOIE

A French range of processed cheese.
(See *Processed Cheese*.)

CREME ROYALE

A Danish double crème cheese similar to Crema Dania.
(See *Crema Dania*.)

CREOLE

An American Cottage style cheese enriched with cream, made in Louisiana and popular in New Orleans.
(See *Cottage* and *Cream Cheese*.)

CRESCENZA

This is an Italian stracchino-style cheese. These cheeses are chiefly soft, white and virtually rindless, are designed to be eaten fresh—they are ripened for periods of only ten to fifteen days. Consequently such cheeses are usually so fresh and delicate that they rarely leave Italy. Crescenza is one of the most highly rated—a very rich, full white creamy cheese, so soft textured it can be spread like butter.
(See *Stracchino*.)

CROTTIN DE CHAVIGNOL

A French chèvre or goat's milk cheese from the Berry province with quite a ferocious reputation. These cheeses have a bloomy natural rind, brownish to dark grey depending on age. They are made in the shape of small 60 g (2 oz) balls. The interiors are soft and cream white when young but darken as they mature. Such cheeses are matured for between two weeks and up to three months. The traditional aged cheeses are extremely pungent and powerful in taste; their aroma is correspondingly rank—most certainly an acquired taste. The young cheeses are, of course, far milder. This cheese is also known as Chavignol from the town where it is made. Crottin simply means 'horse dung'—it refers to the appearance of the cheese, not its taste! (Although people unmoved by its charms might not agree.)
(See *Chèvres*.)

CUMIN CHEDDAR

A flavoured natural Cheddar cheese made in Queensland and South Australia, this is a smooth, firm bodied semi-matured Cheddar with spicy, whole cumin seeds adding a richly piquant flavour.
(See *Cheddar*.)

DAISY

(See American *Cheddars*.)

DAMENKASE

A very mild and bland cheese more commonly known as Butter Cheese. The name means 'ladies' cheese'.
(See *Butter Cheese*.)

DANABLU

Country of origin: Denmark.

Background: Also known as Danish Blue, this is one of the most widely distributed Danish blue-veined cheeses. Danablu is modelled on the French Roquefort, although it is made from cow's milk rather than ewe's milk. The other internationally marketed Danish blue vein is Mycella, a copy of Gorgonzola.

Description: Full size, Danablu generally appears as a flat, cylindrical cheese weighing 2.5-3 kg (6-7 lb) with a diameter of 20 cm (8 in) and a height of 10 cm (4 in). It is also made in rectangular and square shapes.
Consumer portions are marketed in 125 g ($\frac{1}{4}$ lb), 250 g ($\frac{1}{2}$ lb) and 30 g (1 oz) pieces, wrapped in foil or clear film. The cheese is also supplied in circular and rectangular plastic cups containing 125-250 g ($\frac{1}{4}$-$\frac{1}{2}$ lb). Danablu has a thin, white to yellowish-white, slightly greasy surface and a creamy-white interior with delicate blue veining, the result of inoculation with the *Penicillium roqueforti* spore. It is soft-textured, with a creamy consistency, being both spreadable and sliceable. Danablu is, however, a stronger-tasting blue vein than

its companion Mycella, having a sharp, distinctive, piquant flavour, sometimes over-salty.

Wines: Red wines, clarets, burgundies.
Serve: Danablu can be used as a dessert cheese, served with blue grapes or walnuts; in salads or as a cocktail snack on a small square of rye bread with a grape or walnut.
Fat content: 50 per cent (minimum).
Type: Blue vein.
Aroma: Unpronounced, slight smell of mould.

DANBO

Country of origin: Denmark.

Background: This cheese is a member of the Danish family of Samsoe cheeses, Denmark's most popular cheese type. It used to be known as Danish Steppe cheese.

Description: Danbo, made from cow's milk, is made in a flat square measuring 25 cm by 25 cm (10 in) by 7.5 cm (3 in) thick. The rind is dry and yellowish and is sometimes covered with a red or yellow coloured wax.
Danbo has a firm, supple texture with a limited number of small and regularly shaped holes. It is mild, bland and buttery to the taste, faintly sweetish and nut-like. Its flavour sharpens with age. The cheese is usually marketed after maturing for up to five months. Danbo is also made with caraway seeds when it is known as King Christian IX. A Danbo with a 20 per cent fat content is available and is one of the most popular low fat cheeses sold outside Denmark.

Wines: Light whites and reds; beer; also cider.
Serve: A good all-purpose table cheese. Children like it because of its mildness.
Fat content: 45 per cent.
Type: Bland/buttery.
Aroma: Unpronounced.

DANISH CHEF

A range of Danish processed cheese in flavourings varying from shrimp to horseradish.
(See Processed Cheese.)

DANISH FONTINA

A Danish copy of the Italian cheese Fontina. The cheese has a red wax rind (unlike the Italian).
(See Fontina.)

DANISH SAINT PAULIN

A mild flavoured cheese originally modelled on the French Port Salut. The Danish version is creamy and buttery but less sweet than the French and has a sharper tang.
(See Port Salut and Saint Paulin.)

DAUPHIN

A version of Maroilles—a strong smelling and pungent tasting French washed rind cheese.
(See Maroilles.)

DELICE DE SAINT-CYR

A French triple crème cheese made in 12 cm (5 in) disc shapes just over 2.5 cm (1 in) thick. The cheese is matured for three weeks and develops a light white rind which can be spotted with reddish pigmentation. The cheese has a fat content of 75 per cent, giving it an extremely rich, luscious and creamy flavour with a slight undertone of nuts.
(See Triple Crèmes.)

DEMI-SEL

Country of origin: France.

Background: A fresh, unripened cheese from Normandy, similar to Petit Suisse. However, it has a lower fat content and a little salt is added to it. The name refers to its low salt content.

Description: Demi-Sel is made in the shape of a small white square measuring 7.5 by 7.5 cm (3 in) and 2.5 cm (1 in) thick. The cheese is usually marketed wrapped in foil. It has no rind and is smooth, creamy-textured and exquisitely mild-flavoured with a faint sourish tinge. Like Petit Suisse it should always be eaten fresh.

Wines: Can be eaten with tea or coffee or hock-style light white wines.
Serve: Snacks; Demi-Sel's soft texture makes it ideal for spreading on sandwiches.
Fat content: 45 per cent.
Type: Fresh, unripened.
Aroma: Unpronounced.

DERBY

Country of origin: Great Britain (England).

Background: One of what the English call the nine 'champion' cheeses of England (the others are Cheddar, Double Gloucester, Cheshire, Caerphilly, Wensleydale, Leicester, Lancashire and Stilton). Derby was the first English cheese to be factory produced. This happened in 1870 when a group of Derbyshire farmers established a creamery or cheese factory. For centuries until then the cheese had been made in farms throughout Derbyshire.

Description: Derby is a close-textured cheese, slightly flaky, of a pale honey colour. Young Derbys (cheeses matured for between six and eight weeks) are mild and pleasant tasting; when matured for six months they develop a more pronounced tang. Derby is a pleasant, undemanding type of cheese. It lacks Cheddar's character, being a lesser member of the same family.
  Derby Sage is a variant—a Derby cheese that has had fresh sage leaves added to it. This gives it a greenish hue, making it unusual and attractive on display. The sage adds to the cheese a subtle, fragrant flavouring.

Wines: Light reds and dry whites; beer.
Serve: General snack-type cheese.
Fat content: 45 per cent.
Type: Cheddar.
Aroma: Unpronounced.

DOLCELATTE

An Italian blue vein cheese considered a milder, more delicate flavoured Gorgonzola. (See *Gorgonzola*.)

DOMIATI

Country of origin: Egypt.

Background: This cheese is known in many Middle East countries and is extremely popular in Egypt. Like Feta, to which it can be compared, it is a 'pickled' cheese— that is, it is matured in a brine solution which gives it a sharp, salty tang.

Description: Domiati is made in small 7.5 cm (3 in) squares about 2.5 cm (1½ in) deep, or in cylinder shapes up to 12.5 cm (5 in) in diameter. The cheese is sometimes marketed fresh without undergoing a maturing period in brine. At this stage it is mildly salty to the taste, white in colour and has no openings in its surface.
  When fully matured, which is usually for a period of up to eight months, its colour darkens and the cheese acquires a strongly pronounced salty flavour. The cheese is made from whole or skimmed cow's milk, sometimes from buffalo's milk. A similar Egyptian cheese is Kareish.

Wines: Light white and reds.
Serve: Use in a similar fashion to Feta, in hors-d'oeuvres, crumbled into salads, etc.
Fat content: 30-40 per cent.
Type: Pickled cheese.
Aroma: Noticeable smell of brine.

DOUBLE CREMES

Country of origin: France.

Background: The French have been making double crème cheeses for nearly 100 years. During this period they have enjoyed increasing popularity and now are made throughout Europe. All these cheeses have a 60 per cent fat content, defined on their packaging as 60

per cent *matière grasse*. This means that butterfat accounts for 60 grams out of every 100 grams of cheese. The next step up from a double crème is a triple crème, which is defined as having a 75 per cent fat content. Some cheeses with 70 or 72 per cent fat content are obviously on the borderline, but are still classed as double crèmes.

Description: Double crèmes are often made in small cylinder or disc shapes weighing around 150-210 g (5-7 oz). Many which undergo a two to three-week ripening period have a thin downy 'bloomy' rind. Others, those that do not undergo a ripening process, such as Gervais and Petit Suisse, are rindless. Double crèmes have a soft texture, are easily spreadable and are extremely rich and creamy in flavour with a slightly sourish tinge.

The cheeses, usually packaged in cardboard boxes, are marketed under such names as Excelsior, Fin de Siècle, Parfait and Suprême.

Monsieur, La Bouille, Fol Amour and Caprice des Dieux are Camembert/Brie style double crèmes, as are the Danish cheeses Crema Dania and Crema Royale. The last two can almost be classed as triple crèmes as they have a fat content of 72 per cent.

Cheeses such as Blue Castello, Bavarian Blue and Duet, all with a fat content of 70 per cent, are also variations of double crèmes but are noticeably different as they have been given a blue veining.

Wines: Light but fruity reds and sweet white wines; light rosés; can be taken equally well with coffee.
Serve: These cheeses go well with fresh fruit such as apples or strawberries. Varieties such as Petit Suisse can be sprinkled with fine sugar and served as a dessert. Gervais is marketed with fruit flavourings.
Fat content: 60-72 per cent.
Type: Double crèmes.
Aroma: Unpronounced.

DOUBLE GLOUCESTER

Country of origin: Great Britain (England).
Background: There used to be two types of this cheese—a Single and Double Gloucester—the Double so called because it was twice the size of its brother. The Single no longer exists but the Double Gloucester is very much alive and well and is considered one of the great English cheeses. Charles Lamb reckoned it to be the best supper cheese in the world. And they thought so highly of it in Gloucester in times past that it was the practice on festive occasions to garland large Gloucesters with flowers and carry them in triumphant procession through the local villages.

Description: The cheese used to be made from the milk of Gloucester cattle but the breed is almost extinct. There is only one farmer in Gloucestershire now making cheese from this milk and in an extremely small way. Double Gloucester is nowadays made from full cream milk in any of the bordering counties of Gloucestershire such as Somerset, Wiltshire and Dorset.

It is made in the traditional cylindrical shapes weighing from 4.5 kg to 15 kg (10-34 lb) or in rindless blocks weighing up to 20 kg (45 lb). The cheese is also sold in small vacuum packed pieces. Double Gloucester is straw yellow in colour, has a close, firm texture and a full, clean and mellow flavour—a smooth, mature cheese which is ready for eating after maturing for three to four months.

Wines: Any full-bodied red wine but also combines with a pint of beer.
Serve: End of meals; an excellent slicing cheese for sandwiches; can be used with jam, honey or pickles; will also blend pleasantly with a fresh fruit salad and cream.
Fat content: 45 per cent.
Type: Cheddar.
Aroma: Unpronounced.

DOUX DE MONTAGNE

This is part of the range of French mountain cheeses produced in the Pyrenees. Pyrénées is the general name for this style of cheese but many have individual names as well. The best known is Chilberta. Doux de Montagne (sometimes known as Doux de Campagne) is a variety with the colour and shape of a loaf of

Derby (left) Double Gloucester (right)

rye bread. It is a firm textured cheese with a rich, aromatic flavour, not overstrong but still tangy and distinctive.
(See *Chilberta*.)

DUET

A Danish blue vein similar to Blue Castello and Bavarian Blue—a double crème cheese with a moulded surface and blue veining. The cheese has a fat content of 70 per cent.
(See *Blue Veins*.)

DUNLOP

Country of origin: Great Britain (Scotland).

Background: This is one of Scotland's national cheeses, named after a small town in Ayrshire where it was first made in the seventeenth century.

Description: Dunlop is a Cheddar-style cheese, creamy white in colour, essentially mild with a buttery taste. When fully ripened and stored well it develops quite a sharp aftertaste, but it is normally a mild, creamy type of cheese. It is matured for six to eight weeks and is good for toasting.

By the time the cheese reaches its overseas markets it has become more matured and consequently more full-flavoured and pronounced in taste.

Wines: Light dry whites such as rieslings or hocks; light reds; more full-bodied wines such as a muscat or a heavy burgundy are better suited to a mature Dunlop; it will also go with cocktails and spirits.
Serve: End of meals or as a cocktail snack; young Dunlops make good toasting cheeses.
Fat content: 45 per cent.
Type: Cheddar.
Aroma: Unpronounced.

DUTCH CHEESE

(See *Cottage Cheese*.)

EDAM

Country of origin: Holland.

Background: Next to Gouda, this is Holland's most famous cheese export. It takes its name from a town in north Holland which was shipping Edam cheeses to the world in the 17th century. Today Edam accounts for 16 per cent of Holland's total cheese production.

Description: Edam is one of the most distinctive-looking of cheeses—a shiny red ball with a flattened top and bottom. The red surface is the result of the cheese being coated with a paraffin wax. Beneath the wax is a very thin natural rind. The interior is pale yellow, firm but supple textured. Edam, made from cow's milk, has less fat content than Gouda which makes it a slightly harder cheese. The cheese is matured for three to four months.

Edam is a mild, bland, clean tasting cheese, buttery with a faintly acidulous aftertaste. The cheese is usually sold in 1.8 kg (4 lb) ball shapes; loaf shapes are also available.

Varieties of Edam are Baby Edam weighing between 880 g and 1100 g (2-2¼ lb); Commissie, a double Edam weighing between 3 and 4.5 kg (7-10 lb); and Middebare, up to 6.5 kg (14½ lb). All these varieties can be spiced with cumin seed which gives them an extra tang.

Dutch Mature Edam is an Edam that has undergone a longer maturing process (up to a year) and as a result is a much stronger tasting cheese. It is harder and drier and slightly more salty in flavour.

Wines: Light dry whites, light reds; with beer.
Serve: A good all purpose snack cheese, easy to slice, good for sandwiches.
Fat content: 40 per cent.

EDELPILZ

This is a German blue vein more commonly known outside its country of origin as German Blue. Edelpilz means 'cultured cheese' in reference to the inoculation process which creates its veining.
(See *German Blue*.)

EKTE

This is the name given to Norwegian whey cheese Gjetöst when it is made exclusively from goat's milk. Gjetöst has only a 10 per cent goat's milk content. *Ekte* means 'genuine' (i.e. goat's milk cheese).
(See *Gjetöst*.)

ELBO

Country of origin: Denmark.

Background: A member of the Danish Samsoe family of cheeses, the staple cheeses of Denmark. Elbo was once known as Brod, or bread cheese.

Description: Elbo is made in a rectangular loaf shape normally about 30 cm (12 in) by 15 cm (6 in). Its rind is dry and may be coated with a red or yellow wax. The cheese has a firm texture with a limited number of small, pea-sized holes, regular in shape; the interior is pure yellow to white.
Elbo is an extremely bland, buttery and mild-tasting cheese.

Wines: Any light red or dry white.
Serve: An all-purpose, standby cheese, its innocuous flavour making it suitable for children, or in sandwiches as a lunchtime or breakfast snack. It goes well with fruits such as apples, pears and bananas.
Fat content: 45 per cent (minimum).
Type: Bland/buttery.
Aroma: Unpronounced.

EMILIANO

A member of the family of Italian Grana cheeses. Such cheeses are matured over a lengthy period—up to two or three years. During this period they become extremely hard and brittle. They are used in cooking as grating cheeses. The best known is Parmesan.
(See *Grana* and *Parmesan*.)

EMMENTALER

Country of origin: Switzerland.

Background: This world-famous cheese is commonly known as Swiss Cheese and is certainly Switzerland's best known contribution to the cheese world. It originated in the Emmental Valley in the Canton of Berne, where versions of it were known in the sixteenth century. As early as the seventeenth century Emmentaler-type cheese was being exported all over the world, and up to the present day it remains Switzerland's major export cheese. Emmentaler is also made in numerous other countries, but the genuine Swiss variety is stamped 'Switzerland'.

Description: Emmentaler is made in very large sizes, individual cheeses can weigh up to 98 kg (220 lb), but they are usually around the 70 kg (160 lb) mark. The cheeses can be 25 cm (10 in) thick and almost 1 m (3 ft) in diameter. Emmentaler is a hard, cooked, pressed cheese which is treated with three types of bacteria during its making process.
It is called a cooked cheese because after the whey is drained from the curd, it is heated and the curd 'cooked' in it. This is done in huge copper kettles some 2 m (6 ft) in diameter. The cheese is then pressed into its giant millstone shape in hoops and immersed in brine for two to three days. It spends another ten days in a cold room and is then placed in a warmer room temperature (between 65° and 70°F). During this time Emmentaler's characteristic holes or 'eyes' begin to appear across its surface. They are caused by the activity of one of the bacteria used to treat the cheese. It generates propionic acid, thus creating gas which expands within the cheese curd.
After this process the cheese undergoes its principal ripening period in a cool, humid atmosphere. This takes a minimum of five to ten months but can be extended up to a year. Emmentaler has a hard rind which varies in colour from rich yellow to brown. The interior is ivory to light yellow, firm but supple and elastic feeling to the touch—easy to cut. The surface is scattered with round holes varying in diameter from 12 mm ($\frac{1}{2}$ in) to 2.5 cm (1 in).

Emmentalers: French (top and right), Swiss (centre), Austrian (left)

Emmentaler tastes mild, smooth and mellow, with a subtle nut-like flavour, faintly sweetish.

While there are numerous versions of Emmentaler on the market, it is generally accepted that the best versions are Swiss. One reliable guide to quality is the holes in the cheese which should be round, varying between the size of a cherry and a walnut. In a well made, mature cheese these holes will shine with a hint of moisture—a process known as 'weeping'.

Wines: Goes well with fruity white wines (traminers, white burgundies).
Serve: Emmentaler is an extremely versatile cheese well suited to a variety of table and cooking purposes. Cubed, it can be used in salads or speared on toothpicks with olives or walnut halves as a cocktail snack. It can be grated to top toasted snacks or to complement fish, chicken, vegetable and egg dishes. Emmentaler is also ideal for use in a traditional cheese fondue.
Fat content: 48 per cent.

EPICURE

A strong, full flavoured mature Cheddar from New Zealand.
(See *Cheddar*.)

EPOISSES

Country of origin: France.

Description: This is a washed rind cheese made in a flat cylinder shape 10 cm (4 in) in diameter and some 5 cm (2 in) thick. The cheese has its rind regularly washed in wine (some varieties are marinated in burgundy marc) which gives it a smooth, brick red finish, firm and springy to the touch. The interior paste is white to creamy yellow in colour, essentially soft textured. Epoisses spends up to three months maturing under humid conditions, usually undergoing washings once a month.

This is a strong flavoured cheese, penetrating, distinctive and pungent when aged. And they are particularly so when flavoured with herbs such as fennel or spices such as pepper.

The aroma matches the taste. Younger Epoisses (under three months) are milder, quite buttery and creamy tasting.

Wines: Full-bodied red wines.
Serve: End of meals.
Fat content: 45-50 per cent.
Type: Strong smelling (when aged).
Aroma: Pronounced (when aged).

ERBO

A popular mild Italian blue vein which is in fact a processed cheese.
(See *Blue Veins*.)

ESROM

Country of origin: Denmark.

Background: This cheese was originally known as Danish Port Salut. It is not really like French Port Salut being stronger tasting, earthier and closer to Tilsit.

Description: Esrom is made in the shape of a flat, rectangular brick 20 cm by 10 cm by 5 cm (8 in by 4 in by 2 in) and weighs 1.25 kg (2½ lb). The cheese is also produced in the same proportions in weights ranging from 250 g to 500 g (½-1 lb). These cheeses are known as Mini Esroms. It is also made in sizes double the normal length.

Esrom, made from cow's milk, has a thin, washed rind with a tendency to be greasy, yellowish to reddish brown in colour. The cheese's texture is butter-firm, quite sliceable, with a limited number of irregularly shaped, rice-sized holes scattered through its interior paste. It is marketed non-waxed (with or without a rind) or waxed, and is normally packaged in aluminium foil.

The cheese is initially mild-flavoured but has a definite earthy aftertaste and a distinctive aroma. Exported cheeses are likely to be fuller-flavoured as they will have matured longer—they can be quite strong, full and pungent in taste.

Versions of Esrom can be spiced with garlic and other herbs, onion and pepper.

Wines: For the young, blander-tasting Esroms light reds; for an older cheese a more full-bodied red wine.
Serve: End of meals or snacks; the cheese slices well and is suitable for sandwiches or hors d'oeuvres with celery, tomatoes or watercress.
Fat content: 45-60 per cent.
Type: Monastery.
Aroma: Full and distinctive when matured.

EXCELSIOR

A French double crème which is ripened for a three week period. The cheese has a thin, bloomy white rind and a soft, richly luscious texture. Excelsior is made in a 250 g (8 oz) cylinder shape some 10 cm (4 in) in diameter and 2.5 cm (1 in) thick. It has a creamy flavour, quite mild and faintly nutty but very rich as befits a cheese with a 72 per cent fat content.
(See *Double Crèmes*.)

FARM

A French form of cottage cheese also known as Fromage à la Pie, Mou, Maigre and Ferme.
(See *Cottage Cheese*.)

FARMER CHEESE

A very simple cottage style cheese which takes the form of a firm white mass. In flavour it is mild, fresh with a faintly sourish tinge. Like all cottage cheeses it has a low fat content.
(See *Cottage Cheese*.)

FETA

Country of origin: Greece.

Background: This is a traditional Greek cheese which appears in various forms all over the Balkans. It is believed to have been developed by shepherds in the mountain area outside Athens.

Description: Feta is a soft, white cheese generally made from ewe's milk (sometimes from goat's milk), which is noted for its sharp and salty taste. It is known as a 'pickled' cheese because it is matured in a brine solution. Feta is a pale creamy white and amorphous in shape —a moist lumpy mass. It is ripened for at least a month but generally no longer than six weeks. The flavour can vary from very pronounced to mildly salty.

Feta should always be bought moist and will be at its best if still floating in brine on purchase. If you find the cheese too sharp and salty, soak the firm, curdy mass in milk to soften the flavour.

Wines: Ouzo, Retsina.
Serve: Feta is used in savouries, hors d'oeuvres and on cheese platters where its salty flavour enhances dark rye breads, stuffed green or black olives, orange segments, slices of fresh pineapple, avocado or melon. It can be used crumbled in stuffings for aubergines, green peppers and vine leaves, or on salads.
Fat content: 40 per cent.
Type: Sheep's milk.
Aroma: Salty.

A brief comparison of other Fetas sold around the world follows.

AMERICAN FETA: This cheese is made from cow's milk and is quite sharp and pronounced in taste.

ATTIKI FETA (Australian): Similar to Bulgarian Feta, being only slightly salty.

BULGARIAN FETA: Similar to the German, rather sweet and creamy. It is made from sheep's milk.

DANISH FETA: A cheese with a crumbly texture and a quite harsh background taste. It is made from cow's milk.

GERMAN FETA: Almost sweet and quite creamy compared to the other Fetas mentioned here. A mild form of Feta well-suited to the average taste.

Fetas (left to right): Greek, Bulgarian, German

ITALIAN FETA: A good copy of the Greek cheese. It is somewhat drier and coarser than the Bulgarian variety.

PERFECT FETA (Australian): This cheese has a very coarse texture with an open grain, rather sponge-like in appearance. It also is made from cow's milk, but is less salty than the Danish version.

FIN DE SIECLE

Another soft French double crème made in small disc shapes 10 cm (4 in) in diameter and 2.5 cm (1 in) thick. Mild and tasty but very rich and creamy with a 72 per cent fat content.
(See *Double Crèmes*.)

FINNISH EMMENTALER

This is considered one of the best copies of the famous Swiss cheese. Finnish Emmentaler is matured for a longer period than other copies. It is internationally recognised as the best Emmentaler apart from the Swiss original.
(See *Emmentaler*.)

FOL AMOUR

A French double crème Camembert/Brie style cheese from the Champagne area. Made in the shape of a small oval loaf, it has a snow white rind and soft ivory coloured interior paste. Rich and buttery with a 60 per cent fat content—not as complex as a Brie or Camembert but thicker and creamier.
(See *Double Crèmes*.)

FONTAINEBLEAU

A French fresh, unripened cheese with a 75 per cent fat content which also makes it a triple crème cheese.
(See *Triple Crèmes*.)

FONTAL

This is the French version of the Italian cheese Fontina—the French cheese is rather softer, sweeter and more buttery than the Italian original.
(See *Fontina*.)

FONTINA

Country of origin: Italy.

Background: An ancient and highly regarded Italian cheese whose origins go back to the thirteenth century when it was served on the table of the Duke of Savoy. Its full name is Fontina d'Agosta.

Description: Fontina is made in flat wheel shapes which can measure up to 45 cm (18 in) in diameter and nearly 10 cm (4 in) thick. It is a semi-hard cooked cheese made from cow's milk, with a thin natural rind, and is matured for about four months. The cheese's light brown outer rind is covered by a thin wax coat. The interior paste, dotted with a sprinkling of very small holes, is an ivory yellow in colour. Fontina has a firm and supple texture and a light, pleasant aroma.

In flavour the cheese is mild but distinctive with a sweetish nutty tang, complex and involved, highly attractive. A well regarded cheese, it is widely copied. The French version is called Fontal and is softer, sweeter and more buttery. Danish Fontina is somewhat tart or sour by comparison. Swedish Fontina is a more full-flavoured cheese. All three have red waxed rinds, unlike that of the Italian cheese which, as has been mentioned, is light brown. The copies lack the complexity of taste and balance of flavour that makes the Italian Fontina so highly regarded.

Wines: Light red or white wines with definite grape character—semillon, riesling varieties or red burgundy.
Serve: End of meals; well-aged Fontinas can be used as grating cheeses; the cheese also melts easily, making it suitable for fondues.

Fat content: 45-50 per cent.
Type: Bland/buttery/Swiss.
Aroma: Unpronounced.

FONTINELLA

An American version of the Italian cheese Fontina.
(See *Fontina*.)

FORMAGGINI

This is Italian for 'small cheese' and refers to a whole range of small sized Italian cheeses. Such cheeses are sometimes eaten fresh when they are soft, mild, delicate tasting; when fully matured they can become quite sharp.

FOURME D'AMBERT

Country of origin: France.

Background: This is a highly regarded blue vein cheese from the Auvergne province of central France. It is sometimes known as Fourme de Pierre sur Haute and Fourme de Montbrison.

Description: Whatever name it goes under, the cheese appears as a tall cylinder 23 cm (9 in) high and nearly 12.5 cm (5 in) in diameter. It has a greyish rind dotted with reddish and yellow mould patches, beneath which is a creamy white interior with blue veining. The cheese is quite firm and uniform in texture, and not over crumbly. Fourme d'Ambert is ripened in cellars for up to five months—a very full-bodied French bleu with a pronounced pungency and tang, sometimes some bitterness. The cheese is made from cow's milk.

Wines: Full-bodied reds.
Serve: End of meals, snacks.
Fat content: 45 per cent.
Type: Blue vein.
Aroma: Noticeable but not overpronounced mould smell.

FOURME DE PIERRE SUR HAUTE

Another name for the notable French blue vein Fourme d'Ambert—a sharp tasting, strong flavoured cheese.
(See *Fourme d'Ambert*.)

FRENCH EDAM

Edams have been produced in France since 1670 and are often made in the shape of a rectangular loaf. A supple and firm textured cheese, softer, more buttery and sweeter than the Dutch cheese it is based on.
(See *Edam*.)

FRENCH GRUYERE

This French version of the world famous Swiss cheese is less sweet than the original on which it is based, sharper, spicier, full and fruity flavoured.
(See *Gruyère*.)

FRESCO

Another name for the stracchino style Italian cheese Milano.
(See *Stracchino* and *Milano*.)

FRIESIAN

Country of origin: Holland.

Background: This is a spiced cheese which comes from Friesland, a northern province of Holland, near the Zuider Zee.

Description: This cheese is sometimes spiced with cumin alone, and sometimes a combination of cumin and cloves. Kanter is a third variation which is made without the addition of any spices.

Friesian has a flat cylindrical shape with sharp edges. The rind is tough and hard, a brownish yellow in colour; the interior is firm textured. The cheese is made in various weights up to about 9 kg (20 lb). It is made in two versions; one from whole cow's milk, the other from skimmed milk. This factor affects the fat content.

Friesian, in many ways, is similar to Leyden, both highly rated spiced cheeses. In taste Friesian is pleasantly tangy and spicy, not overstrong, attractively distinctive. The cheese takes six months to develop its full flavour and aroma.

Wines: The Dutch recommend it with Scotch; will also go with fruity reds, dry whites and beer.
Serve: End of meals; sandwich snacks.
Fat content: 20-40 per cent.
Type: Spiced.
Aroma: Noticeable full aroma of cloves.

FROMAGE A LA CREME

A variety of Fromage Blanc, a French fresh, unripened cheese eaten with cream and sugar.
(See *Fromage Blanc*.)

FROMAGE BLANC

An extremely simple French, unripened fresh cheese, basically sour milk placed in a muslin bag and left to drain of its whey for a short while. It is then eaten with pepper and salt.

Variations include Fromage à la Crème, the same cheese but eaten with cream with sugar sprinkled over it, and Coeur à la Crème. The latter differs only in that the muslin draining bag is placed in a heart shaped wicker basket which moulds the cheese into the shape from which it takes its name.

There are numerous varieties of French fresh, unripened cheese. Demi-Sel is small, moist, creamier and a trifle more complex than the three preceding; the famous Petit Suisse is in fact an unripened double crème best eaten with sugar and strawberries. There are even unripened triple crème cheeses such as Fontainbleau.

Generally all French fresh, unripened cheeses are more sour and tangy tasting than fresh cheeses made outside Europe.
(See *Cottage* and *Cream Cheese*; also *Double and Triple Crèmes*.)

FROMAGE FONDU

The name under which a great range of French processed cheese is marketed via a variety of brand names.
(See *Processed Cheese*.)

FROMAGE FORT

This is the generic name for a range of French cheeses which are beaten and mashed into a paste-like consistency. The cheeses are then flavoured with a variety of herbs—parsley, tarragon and pepper, for example. Wine is then added and the cheese is sealed in a crock and left for periods ranging from two weeks to three months. The result is something noted for its powerful and penetrating flavour and matching aroma. Popular as a miner's snack in some parts of France—not usually commercially marketed but produced in homes.

FYNBO

Country of origin: Denmark.

Background: A member of the Samsoe family of Danish cheeses, this cheese takes its name from the island of Fynbo where it was first made.

Description: Fynbo is made in the shape of a flat round disc with rounded sides and edges. Full size, the cheese measures 31 cm (12½ in) in diameter and weighs approximately 6-7 kg

(13-16 lb). It is also produced in sizes weighing from 250 g ($\frac{1}{2}$ lb) to 13 kg (30 lb).

Fynbo has a dry yellowish rind which may be covered with either red or yellow wax. Its interior varies from pure yellow to white in colour, is firm and supple and contains a limited number of regularly shaped pea-sized holes. The cheese has a mild and buttery flavour, slightly aromatic.

Tropefynbo (Tropical Fynbo) is also made. This is the same shape as Fynbo, but has smaller dimensions and weighs only 3.5 kg (8 lb). It has a firmer consistency with a thicker rind designed to enable it to withstand high temperatures.

Tropefynbo is red or yellow waxed and is marked with either a letter 'T' or the word 'Trope'. It is normally packaged in red cellophane. In taste it is somewhat sharper than the normal Samsoe range because of its higher salt content.

A Mini-Fynbo weighs 250 g ($\frac{1}{2}$ lb).

Wines: Light red and rosé wines; dry whites.
Serve: Fynbo, like all members of the Samsoe family, is a useful all-purpose cheese. It slices easily and is therefore ideal for sandwiches; its blandness also makes it popular with children. The cheese goes well with apples, cherries and spring onions.
Fat content: 45 per cent (minimum).
Type: Bland/buttery.
Aroma: Unpronounced.

GAMMELOST

Country of origin: Norway.

Background: This traditional cheese is reputed to have been made since Viking times—in fact, its name means 'old cheese'. Gammelost is made in the counties of Hardanger and Sogu in western Norway.

Description: Gammelost is a highly pungent combination of a sour skimmed milk cheese and a blue vein. It is usually made in 15 cm (6 in) high cylinder shapes up to 15 cm (6 in) in diameter, weighing up to 4 kg (9 lb). Gammelost is both surface ripened and internally moulded. The rind is brownish in colour, rough and uneven, while the semi-soft interior is browny-yellow with a bluish-green tint of veining.

After the cheese has been ripened for about a month it is stored in straw that has been impregnated with the juice of juniper berries.

All in all, a set of circumstances that makes for a very pungent and pronounced tasting cheese, a blue vein like no other, and very much an acquired taste.

Wines: Full-bodied reds.
Serve: End of meals.
Fat content: 4-5 per cent.
Type: Blue vein.
Aroma: Pronounced smell of mould.

GAPERON

Country of origin: France.

Background: This is an old French cheese from the Auvergne which takes its name from the dialect word for buttermilk—*gap* or *gape*. In past times the number of these cheeses hanging in a farmhouse kitchen reflected the farmer's wealth and helped him marry off his daughter. The cheese is also known as Gapron.

Description: This fairly off-beat country cheese comes in a flattened ball shape about 9 cm (3$\frac{1}{2}$ in) in diameter and 7.5 cm (3 in) high. It can be made from cow's milk, skimmed milk or buttermilk and has a low fat content. Gaperon, which is flavoured with garlic, has a bluish-grey uneven rind which covers a cream white, soft textured interior paste. The cheeses are ripened under mainly dry conditions for about two months.

Gaperon is quite a full flavoured cheese, distinctive, with an attractively spiced garlic tang.

Wines: Full-bodied reds.
Serve: Snacks; an unusual and distinctive cheese to serve on a cheese board.
Fat content: 30 per cent.
Type: Spiced.
Aroma: Noticeable.

GARLIC CHEDDAR

Natural Garlic Cheddar is an Australian Cheddar variety made at Mount Gambier, South Australia. It is a full-bodied, matured Cheddar with a smooth creamy texture and a delicate garlic flavour.
(See *Cheddar*.)

GERMAN BLUE

Country of origin: Germany.

Background: This is a blue vein cheese, also known as Edelpilz. Edelpilz means 'cultured cheese' in reference to the inoculation process which creates its veining.

Description: German Blue is a yellow to white cheese with bluish-green veining and the typically soft, slightly crumbly texture of cheeses of this type. It is made in loaf shapes or in cylindrical forms about 15 cm (6 in) high. All blue veins are strong, tangy cheeses but the degree of robustness and tanginess of flavour varies considerably. German Blue is piquant and full-flavoured but not harshly pronounced or over-salty—a well-balanced and harmonised cheese.

Wines: Strong, full-bodied reds.
Serve: End of meals; crumbled and mixed into salads; as a dessert mixed with cream or mayonnaise and filled into pear halves; use in baked potatoes instead of sour cream and chives.
Fat content: 45 per cent.
Type: Blue vein.
Aroma: Noticeable smell of mould.

GERMAN EDAM

A copy of the Dutch cheese and at the very bland end of the Edam range. A soft, plastic, rectangular shaped cheese, mild and buttery with a rubbery texture. It is sweeter than most Edams, apart from the French, and almost white in colour.
(See *Edam*.)

GERMAN GOUDA

This copy of the famous Dutch cheese is bland, almost tasteless—rather like eating lightly flavoured butter.
See *Gouda*.)

GEROME

Country of origin: France.

Background: This is one of the oldest of the French cheeses and is related to Münster.

Description: Gérômé is a soft, washed-rind cheese ripened for periods of between one and three months in cellars with a high degree of humidity to promote bacterial growth.
Made from cow's milk, this surface-ripened cheese is made in disc shapes up to 20 cm (8 in) in diameter and 5 cm (2 in) thick. Gérômé has a reddish rind, soft, ivory yellow interior paste and a very strong, gamy, pungent aroma. Its flavour is strong too, very spicy, tangy and pronounced—not a cheese for lovers of the mild and bland. Versions spiced with caraway and cumin seeds are also made.
Jerome, a German version, has an orange coloured rind and an almost pure white interior dotted with holes. It is every bit as pungent smelling and tasting as the French variety.

Wines: Strong, full-bodied reds; also beer.
Serve: End of meals; on bread as a snack.
Fat content: 45-50 per cent.
Type: Monastery/strong smelling.
Aroma: Pronounced, pungent.

GERVAIS

A popular range of French fresh double crème cheeses. Gervais has been known since 1850. The cheese is pure white in colour and has a buoyant texture; the flavour is rich and creamy with a lightly sourish tinge. Varieties are marketed with fruit flavourings.
(See *Double Crèmes*.)

GEX

A tangy, full flavoured French blue vein of good quality, very savoury but can be a trifle bitter. The cheese is also called Bleu de Sept-moncel and Bleu du Haut Jura.
(See *Bleus*.)

GJETOST

Country of origin: Norway.

Background: Gjetöst has been Norway's national cheese for more than a hundred years. The name means 'goat cheese', but today is something of a misnomer as Gjetöst is generally made with only 10 per cent goat's milk content; the other 90 per cent is made up of cow's milk.

Description: This is a genuinely offbeat cheese, unlike any other and uncheeselike in taste and appearance. It is made from the liquid whey rather than the curd. The whey is boiled, then milk sugar (lactose) and cream are added. The result is a cheese that looks like a large chunk of caramel fudge. It does not undergo a ripening process.
 Gjetöst is usually marketed in 250 g ($\frac{1}{2}$ lb) and 500 g (1 lb) rectangular blocks; it comes foil wrapped. It is a light brown in colour throughout (it has no rind) and has a firm, close texture.
 In taste it is sweetish, mild, fudgelike, even vaguely fishy—with undertones of caramel-flavoured condensed milk. It is very much an acquired taste. Norwegian Dairies say its 'character reflects the healthy outdoor life' of the country.
 When Gjetöst is made entirely from goat's milk it is known as Ekte (genuine) Gjetöst. Mysost is a version made entirely from cow's milk.
 The fact that lactose is added to it makes the cheese a good energy source, a useful cheese to have around on walking holidays and similar outdoor pursuits.

Wines: Goes best with coffee or hot chocolate, but will also combine with spirits such as freezer-cold gin.

Serve: The Norwegians recommend it for breakfast, cut in wafer-thin slices with a cheese slicer and served on bread, crispbread, biscuits, raisin bread or crackers.
Fat content: 38 per cent.
Type: Whey.
Aroma: Unpronounced.

GLARNERKASE

A name by which the Swiss spiced grating cheese Sapsago is also known. Other names include Glarenkäse, Glaren Schabziger, Green Cheese.
(See *Sapsago*.)

GOLD'N RICH

A semi-soft American Cheddar which is particularly popular in mid-west America.
(See American *Cheddars*.)

GORGONZOLA

Country of origin: Italy.

Background: Gorgonzola, named after a village near Milan, has been made in Italy's Po Valley since the ninth century.

Description: This is Italy's most famous blue vein cheese, ranking alongside the English Stilton and the French Roquefort as one of the top three blue veins in the world.
 The cheese is made in cylindrical shapes standing some 20 cm (8 in) high and about 30 cm (12 in) in diameter. It is softer and creamier than Stilton and Roquefort and the characteristic veining which mottles its interior, the result of inoculation with the *Penicillium glaucum* spore, is greenish rather than blue.
 Gorgonzolas are generally matured for from four to six months, but sometimes up to a year. Long maturation increases their robustness of

Gorgonzola (photo by Russell Cockayne)

flavour considerably, but all are strong, rich, creamy and pungent tasting cheeses, more creamy and less salty than most other blues. They also have a noticeably pungent aroma.

Wines: Full-bodied reds, ports, heavy red burgundies; if you are lucky enough to encounter a young Gorgonzola, try it with a dry traminer/riesling-style white and crisp apples.
Serve: End of meals with fruit, especially apples or pears; in a crunchy wholegrain brown bread sandwich with slices of apple as part of the filling; as a salad dressing; grilled in hot jacket potatoes; as a topping for a charcoal steak.
Fat content: 48-50 per cent.
Type: Blue vein.
Aroma: Pungent and full.

GOUDA

Country of origin: Holland.

Background: More than half of the Netherlands' cheese production is given over to Gouda—one of the two best-known Dutch cheeses in the world (the other is Edam). It takes its name from the town where it originated in the thirteenth century.

Description: Goudas are made in the shape of small wheels with rounded sides and flat tops and bottoms. They come in various sizes, one of the most common being 35 cm (14 in) in diameter and 10-12.5 cm (4-5 in) thick.
The cheese has a waxed red or yellow rind. The interior is straw-yellow, firm-feeling to the touch, its surface dotted with small and unevenly-shaped holes. Gouda is a mild-tasting cheese, pleasantly creamy and buttery.
Spiced Gouda is a variety flavoured with cumin seed, which makes it quite tangy. It also has a firmer texture.
Dutch Mature Gouda has undergone a longer maturing process of up to a year (normal Goudas are matured for between three to four months) and is noticeably different in taste and appearance. The rind is a darker yellow, almost brown, and the dryness of the rind can extend a good half-inch into the cheese. Mature Gouda has a quite pronounced, distinctive aftertaste, cloying to

the palate and resembling a mild, unsalted Cheddar.
There are also smoked and salt-free versions of Gouda.
'Baby' Goudas are made in weights varying from 310 g (10 oz) to 620 g (20 oz).
In the USA the term 'fresh' Gouda is used to denote the young Goudas as opposed to the mature ones—even though the 'fresh' Goudas have been matured for between three and four months.

Wines: Gouda blends pleasantly with almost any wine and you can also drink beer with it—a cheese for all seasons. The spiced variety is better suited to heavy-bodied reds such as cabernet sauvignon and shiraz styles, and dry rather than sweet whites.
Serve: A good bland all-purpose table cheese —try it with pickles or jam.
Fat content: 48 per cent.
Type: Bland/buttery.
Aroma: Unpronounced.

GOURMANDISE

A widely marketed and popular brand of French processed cheese.
(See *Processed Cheese*.)

GOURNAY

Another name for a type of Neufchâtel—a small, soft, bloomy rind cream cheese which has been made in Normandy for centuries.
(See *Neufchâtel*.)

GRADDOST

Country of origin: Sweden.

Background: Gräddost means 'butter cheese' in Swedish and is essentially a bland and buttery style cheese with a high fat content which relates it to double crèmes.

Description: This is a popular, mass marketed Swedish cheese made in varying sizes in cylinder shapes and rectangular blocks. The cheese has a waxed or paraffined yellow rind with an open textured interior dotted with small, irregularly shaped holes. Gräddost is matured for some two months and is firm textured, supple and easily sliced. It has a fresh, clean, buttery taste, smooth and mild.

Wines: Light reds and whites; goes with beer.
Serve: A good all-purpose snack cheese; blends well with fruit.
Fat content: 60 per cent.
Type: Bland and buttery (its high fat content also puts it in the category of double crèmes.
Aroma: Unpronounced.

GRANA

Country of origin: Italy.

Background: Grana is not one cheese, but several. The name refers to a group of hard, granular Italian cheeses developed about A.D. 1200 in the Po Valley.

Description: All Grana cheeses have in common a hard granular texture, a sharp, biting, pronounced flavour and excellent keeping qualities, even in hot climates. This type of cheese also travels well, which helps make it one of Italy's major cheese export items.
   Grana cheese is principally used for grating. The oldest and best-known member of the group is Parmesan. Grana cheeses are often made in thick wheel shapes up to 45 cm (18 in) in diameter. Their colour is straw-yellow but they are often coated with a blackish mixture of oil and umber.
   Varieties include Lombardo, Lodigiano, Emiliano and Asiago.
   Grana cheeses can be aged for up to four years, which makes them extremely hard and brittle, ideal for grating, but young cheeses (aged under a year) can be used as table cheeses.

Wines: Any full-bodied red such as Chianti.
Serve: Grated onto dishes such as spaghetti bolognaise and minestrone.
Fat content: Approximately 30-35 per cent.

Type: Extra hard grating cheeses.
Aroma: Unpronounced.
(See *Parmesan.*)

GRANA PADANO

One of the numerous range of Italian Grana cheeses of the same *genre* as Parmesan. The cheese is made in large cylinders and can weigh up to 40 kg (16 lb). It has a hard, granular texture and a fragrant, delicate flavour. Such cheeses can be aged up to two years and are widely used for grating. Younger versions can be used as table cheeses. The cheese has a relatively low fat content of 32 per cent.
(See *Parmesan.*)

GRAND VATEL

A French triple crème cheese similar to Délice de Saint-Cyr.
(See *Double Crèmes.*)

GRAPPE

This is a popular French processed cheese distinguished by the fact that grape skins and pips form its rind. In the USA it is known as Grappe but its correct name is La Grappe.
(See *Processed Cheese.*)

GREEN CHEESE

More commonly known as Sapsago, the Swiss grating cheese. It is sometimes called Green Cheese because of its colour.
(See *Sapsago.*)

GRUNLAND

A German range of processed cheeses.
(See *Processed Cheese.*)

GRUYERE

Country of origin: Switzerland.

Background: Next to Emmentaler, Gruyère is Switzerland's best known and most widely exported cheese. It is very old, some authorities believing it to date back to the twelfth century. It takes its name from the valley of Gruyère in the Canton of Fribourg.

Description: Gruyère is similar to Emmentaler but is made in smaller sizes and has a stronger flavour. It is usually made in large wheels measuring just over 75 cm (30 in) in diameter and 10 cm (4 in) thick. Gruyères can weigh between 35-40 kg (78-90 lb).

Like Emmentaler it is a hard, cooked pressed cheese. Gruyère has a hard outer rind the texture of pressed biscuits and a firm but supple interior, light yellow to amber in colour, scattered with small holes caused by expanding gases released by bacterial growth during the curing process.

The holes, or 'eyes' as they are sometimes known, are much smaller than those found in Emmentaler. In Gruyère the holes vary between pea and cherry stone size. The cheese takes about six months to ripen, sometimes longer.

Gruyère's taste varies with its age but, like Emmentaler, it is nut-flavoured, with a sweetish lingering aftertaste, but sharper, more acid and slightly saltier. As Gruyère has a higher fat content, it is also a richer, creamier-tasting cheese than Emmentaler.

The older the cheese the fuller, deeper and richer tasting it will be.

Wines: Aged dry whites or dry reds such as cabernet sauvignons.
Serve: End of meals as a table cheese; in fondues, quiches, as a surface topping for dishes such as veal cordon bleu and onion soup.
Fat content: 48 per cent.
Type: Swiss.
Aroma: Noticeable smell of nuts.

GRUYERE DE BEAUFORT

An ancient French cheese similar to Gruyère but richer and more buttery tasting. This cheese is more commonly known as Beaufort. (See *Beaufort*.)

GRUYERE DE COMTE

A type of French Gruyère which dates back to the thirteenth century. The cheese is more commonly known as Comté. (See *Comté*.)

HALOUMY

Country of origin: Greece.

Background: This cheese, found in many parts of the Mediterranean area, is related to Feta. Like Feta, it is a so-called 'pickled' cheese, being matured in brine.

Description: Haloumy appears as a firmish, putty-like mass, creamy white in colour and with a string-like consistency to its texture. When it is made the curd is dipped in hot whey, kneaded, rolled out and folded with mint leaves or herbs between the layers. It is matured in brine which gives it a sharp salty tang; this is usually not as pronounced as in Feta, the mint flavouring the cheese acquires offsetting the sharpness of the salt.

Wines: Fruity reds or Greek wines like Retsina and Ouzo.
Serve: Haloumy can be used in a variety of ways to add a slightly unusual flavouring; in salads, pastries or on a grilled steak; also eaten fondue-style by being dipped into hot water and drawn out in strings.
Fat content: 40 per cent.
Type: Sheep's milk.
Aroma: Unpronounced.

HAND

Country of origin: USA.

Background: This cheese is the American descendant of a type originally made in several European countries and particularly popular in Germany. It takes its name from the way it used to reach its final shape—hand moulded. First made in America by farmers of German descent in Pennsylvania, it is still made on some farms but is also factory-produced in New York, Illinois and Wisconsin.

Description: Hand is a small cheese, which can be pungent and powerful in smell and taste. It is made from skimmed sour milk, sometimes mixed with whole milk, often in the shape of a flat disc 5-7.5 cm (2-3 in) in diameter. The cheese is surface-ripened for six to eight weeks before marketing by the outside being smeared with a broth of mould-producing bacteria. Hand has a supple, rubbery texture with a smooth surface which can be golden yellow to reddish-brown in colour; the interior is usually a pale glassy yellow.

Although younger cheeses can be mild tasting, all things considered Hand cheese can be classed as an acquired taste. A well ripened cheese is extremely pronounced in taste and aroma.

Hand is quite nutritious, however, with a low fat level and a high protein content. Caraway seeds are sometimes added to provide an extra tang.

In Germany many varieties of this type of cheese are made, one of the most popular being Harz.

Wines: Eat Hand with beer; the Germans sometimes melt them in beer and drink the mixture.
Serve: As a snack; the Germans often cover them with a mixture of vinegar dressing, paprika and onions.
Fat content: Less than 10 per cent.
Type: Strong smelling.
Aroma: Pronounced.
(See *Sour Curd Cheese*.)

HARZ

Country of origin: Germany.

Background: This is one of a number of German cheeses made from skimmed sour milk. It is made in two areas—the Harz Mountains, where this style of cheese has been eaten since the early part of the nineteenth century, and Mainz, a Rhineland port. The cheese is usually extremely pungent in both taste and aroma, not recommended for intimate dinner parties for guests with delicate palates. Harz is, however, quite nutritious, having a high protein content and a low fat content.

Description: Harz comes in a variety of sizes and shapes. One of the most common is a small disc shape measuring 5 cm (2 in) in diameter and 2.5 cm (1 in) thick.

The cheese has a smooth, golden yellow to reddish-brown surface, a pale, glassy yellow interior and a supple, rubbery texture. It is made in strengths varying from mild to pronounced but all are something of an acquired taste. Even the mild versions would seem quite distinctive to people not used to them. The strong Harz cheeses are extremely so, pungent, powerful and potent in both flavour and aroma.

The American descendant of this type of cheese is Hand, first produced by German farmers in Pennsylvania.

Wines: Harz is often eaten with beer and *in* beer; in Hessen it is eaten with cider.
Serve: Harz enthusiasts coat the cheese with a vinegar-oil dressing, add onions and paprika and enjoy them as a mid-morning snack.
Fat content: Less than 10 per cent.
Type: Strong smelling.
Aroma: Pronounced.
(See *Sour Curd Cheese*.)

HAVARTI

Country of origin: Denmark.

Background: Havarti was once known as Danish Tilsit, having been modelled on the German cheese of that name. Its name was changed in recognition of the work of Hanne Nielson, a nineteenth century pioneer of the Danish cheese industry, Havarti being the name of her farm.

Description: Havarti is made in rectangular loaf shapes weighing 4 kg (9 lb) and measuring 30 cm by 12 cm by 12 cm (12 x 5 x 5 in).

It is also made to the same proportions in weights ranging from 250 g ($\frac{1}{2}$ lb) to about 5 kg (11 lb). Round cheeses weighing about 5 kg (11 lb) are also made. The cheeses can be waxed and usually come foil-wrapped.

Havarti, a washed rind cheese made from cow's milk, has a thin yellowish rind with a tendency to greasiness. Its interior may be any shade from pure yellow to white, and contains numerous irregular rice-sized (sometimes larger) holes. The texture is half-firm, quite sliceable.

The cheese is one of the more full-flavoured of the Danish varieties but its actual strength varies with its age. Bought after its normal two to three months' maturing time it is full and smooth tasting with a piquant aftertaste; older versions acquire a greater pungency of flavour.

Another variety of this cheese is known as Havarti 60 per cent because of its higher fat content. Havarti 60 per cent is a richer, creamier cheese, slightly acid with a tangy aftertaste, becoming stronger with maturity.

Wines: Light dry whites; fruity reds; also goes with beer.
Serve: A good tangy snack cheese which goes well with vegetables such as tomatoes, cucumber, celery and olives.
Fat content: 45 per cent.
Type: Monastery.
Aroma: Noticeably aromatic; can be quite pronounced when aged.

HERRGARDSOST

Country of origin: Sweden.

Background: The name means 'manor cheese' and it has been one of Sweden's most popular cheeses since it first appeared towards the end of last century.

Description: Herrgårdsost is a hard, cooked, pressed cheese made in cylinder shapes about 37.5 cm (15 in) in diameter and 15 cm (6 in) high. The rind is usually coated with a yellow wax; its interior is yellow-white, smooth, close with a small number of round holes. The cheese is made either from partly skimmed cow's milk or from whole cow's milk; it ripens for between three and six months depending on the variety being made. The whole milk version, which is allowed to mature for the longer period, is known as Herrgård Elite.

Herrgårdsost is a Swiss style cheese modelled on Emmentaler. The young cheeses are mild, sweetish tasting with nutty undertones, reminiscent of Emmentaler but less complex and nearer to Jarlsberg in flavour. The older Herrgårdsosts gain in depth of flavour and fullness of taste.

Wines: Light reds or dry whites; beer also goes well.
Serve: Good snack cheese.
Fat content: Up to 45 per cent.
Type: Swiss.
Aroma: Unpronounced.

HERVE

Country of origin: Belgium.

Background: This is a Limburger-style cheese which takes its name from the Hervé area in the province of Liège. Its history goes back to the Middle Ages and it is yet another cheese created by monks.

Description: Hervé is made in cubes about 7.5 cm (3 in) deep. It is a washed rind cheese, surface ripened and cured for up to three months in humid conditions. The cheese is supple feeling and has a thin reddish-brown outer rind. Like Limburger, it is a cheese with a highly pronounced odour. Its taste is also highly pronounced, very strong, pungent and tangy. Hervé is sometimes flavoured with olives, parsley or tarragon.

Remoudou, another Belgian cheese, is similar but is made in larger sizes. It too is pungent in both taste and aroma and highly salted.

Wines: Full-bodied reds.
Serve: End of meals; as a snack with full-flavoured vegetables such as onions.
Fat content: 45 per cent.
Type: Monastery/strong smelling.
Aroma: Pronounced.

HICK-O-RY

One of the most popular of the American smoked cheese range. The cheese is 15 cm (10 in) long with a rectangular cross section 7.5 cm (3 in) by 4 cm (1½ in).
(See *Smoked Cheeses*.)

HOLYLAND

A trade name for an Israeli line of cheeses characterised by being Kosher—rennin is not used as a starter when the cheeses are made.

ILCHESTER

Country of origin: Great Britain (England).

Background: In the last few years the English have adapted a number of their traditional cheeses by adding to them a variety of flavouring ingredients ranging from wine to chives. Ilchester is one of these and comes in three varieties.

Description: The three types of Ilchester are Cheddar with beer, Double Gloucester with cider and Stilton with port. Of these three the Stilton with port is the richest: England's most famous blue-veined cheese, with a rich, pronounced and pungent flavour, mixed with port wine. The Gloucester variety has the mellow, creamy flavour characteristic of the cheese with the cider adding a sweetish undertone. The Cheddar is a mild-tasting cheese flavoured with beer.

Wines: Stilton with port; the Gloucester with cider or a light white wine; the Cheddar with beer.
Serve: The Stilton variety is suitable as a rich dessert cheese; the other two versions of Ilchester can be used in the same manner but are also well suited as snacks.
Fat content: Stilton, 55 per cent; Gloucester and Cheddar, 45 per cent.
Type: Cheddar.
Aroma: Stilton, a mould smell; Gloucester and Cheddar, unpronounced.

INCANESTRATO

Also known as Canestrato or Pecorino Siciliano, this is a sheep's milk cheese from Sicily similar to Pecorino Romano. Well aged versions of this type of cheese are used for grating.
(See *Pecorino Romano*.)

JALAPENO

An unusual spiced cheese named after the famous Mexican 'hot' pepper. The cheese (often a processed Cheddar) has pieces of jalapeno dispersed through it. It is very popular in the south-west and west of the USA.
(See *Spiced Cheeses*.)

JARLSBERG

Country of origin: Norway.

Background: This modern descendant of a traditional Norwegian cheese was developed on the Jarlsberg estate on the western shore of the Oslo fjord, a cheesemaking area for hundreds of years.

Description: Jarlsberg is made in wheel shapes weighing around 9 kg (20 lb). It is a hard, cooked pressed cheese, white to light yellow in colour, its interior liberally scattered with large and irregularly-shaped rounded holes in a similar style to Emmentaler. The cheese has a thick natural rind covered with a yellow wax. The interior is firm, supple, elastic and slightly waxy or rubbery. In many ways Jarlsberg resembles Emmentaler but the Norwegians insist that it is not a copy of the Swiss cheese, but a cheese in its own right. It does not taste like Emmentaler, being sweeter with undertones of nuts but lacking the Swiss cheese's complexity of flavour.

Much Jarlsberg on the market today is packaged in rindless blocks.

Jarlsberg is popular with children and it is generally an excellent family standby. The cheese is made from cow's milk and is matured for three to six months.

Wines: Light dry whites; fruity reds.
Serve: A good all-purpose family cheese; try it on dark buttered bread with slices of tomato and cucumber topped off with filleted anchovy and parsley.
Fat content: 45 per cent.
Type: Swiss.
Aroma: Unpronounced.

JEROME

A German version of the French washed rind cheese Géromé. Jerome has an orange coloured rind and an almost pure white soft interior dotted with holes—a gamy, pungent smelling and tasting cheese.
(See *Géromé*.)

KAMERUKA

(See Australian *Cheddars*.)

KANTER KAAS

This is the spiced Dutch cheese Friesian minus spices. Friesian can be spiced with a combination of cumin and cloves or cumin alone; the cheese is called Kanter when it is made without the addition of any spices whatever.
(See *Friesian*.)

KAREISH

One of Egypt's 'pickled' cheeses. Such cheeses are matured in brine and develop a pronounced salty tang. The best known cheese of this type in Egypt is Domiati.
(See *Domiati* and *Pickled Cheese*.)

KATSCHKAWALJ

A sheep's milk cheese from the Balkans, very similar to the better known Kashkaval.
(See *Kashkaval*.)

KASHKAVAL

Country of origin: Rumania.

Background: Cheeses of this type are made all over the Balkan countries. Katschkawalj is the Bulgarian variety; the Turks make one called Zomma. Kasseri, from Greece, is similar.

Description: This sheep's milk cheese looks like a large millstone-shaped piece of white soap. It can be made in sizes up to 45 cm (18 in) in diameter and about 7.5 cm (3 in) deep. The cheese is matured for between two and three months and has a firm texture, slightly moist with a very thin rind.
Kashkaval has a distinctive and attractive flavour; tangy, almost a gritty background, sourish, 'sheepish' but tasty and appealing. It should never be oversharp or too salty.
Kashkaval is a drawn curd cheese (its curd is placed in hot water and worked and moulded while in a malleable condition). As its curd is cut into small pieces or 'cheddared' during the making process, it is also related to the Cheddar family.

Wines: Dry whites; also combines with beer.
Serve: A tasty, appealing cheese for the cheese board; try it as a snack with French bread and ham.
Fat content: 30 per cent.
Aroma: Noticeable full sheep's milk aroma, rather sourish.
Type: Sheep's milk/Cheddar family.

KASSERI

Country of origin: Greece.

Description: This cheese can be made from sheep's or goat's milk and is similar to Kashkaval but stronger tasting. Kasseri is made in large flat wheels which weigh about 9 kg (20 lb). It is a hard, pressed, uncooked cheese, creamy-white in colour, firm-textured with a few very small holes.
Kasseri is not overstrong in taste but has a pronounced sourish, sheep's milk quality to it.
An American version of Kasseri is milder and quite well regarded.

Wines: Retsina, full-bodied reds.
Serve: End of meals.
Fat content: 40 per cent.
Type: Sheep's milk.
Aroma: Unpronounced.

KAUKAUNA KLUB

A popular American Cheddar style cheese sold
in china crocks. This style of cheese is known
as coldpack cheese and is very spreadable.
(See American *Cheddars* and
Coldpack Cheese.)

KEFALOTYRI

This cheese can be made from either sheep's or
goat's milk. It has a noticeable sheep's milk
tang, lightly salty, rather mealy, oily, simple
and attractive. The cheese is firm textured
with a hard rind. Kefalotyri is made in cylinder
shapes about 25 cm (10 in) in diameter. It is
mainly used for grating and cooking. It is
similar to Kasseri (which is somewhat softer)
and Kashkaval. The cheese takes its name
from its shape, which is supposed to resemble a
type of Greek hat.
(See *Kashkaval*.)

KERNHEM

Country of origin: Holland.

Description: This is a flat, cylindrical shaped
cheese with a soft creamy texture which makes
it unsuitable for slicing. The Dutch place this
cheese in a group known as 'meshanger' types
—cheese that sticks to the knife when cut.
Kernhem, which was developed by the Netherlands Institute for Dairy Research, is similar in
style to a Saint Paulin but richer, creamier and
more pronounced tasting. A washed rind
cheese made from cow's milk, it is ripened for
four weeks and made in sizes with a 25 cm
(10 in) diameter, 5 cm (2 in) thick, weighing
1.6 kg (3.5 lb). It has a higher than average
fat content.

Serve: End of meals; snacks.
Wines: Full-bodied reds.
Fat content: 60 per cent.
Type: Monastery.
Aroma: Unpronounced but noticeable.

KING CHRISTIAN IX

A Danish cheese that is a version of Danbo
with caraway seeds—a member of the Samsoe
family of cheeses. It is known as King Christian
IX because it was a great favourite of that
Danish monarch's. Essentially a clean, mild
tasting spiced cheese.
(See *Danbo*)

KLEINKASE

An Austrian cheese the size of, and similar to, a
baby Gouda. A mild, bland, firm textured
cheese.
(See *Gouda*.)

KORB

This is a German type of sour curd cheese—a
range of cheeses noted for their sharpness of
flavour and pungent aroma. The cheeses have
a low fat content and are high in protein but
are very much an acquired taste.
(See *Sour Curd Cheeses*, *Harz* and *Mainz*.)

KRAUTERKASE

A German version of the Swiss grating cheese
Sapsago, notable for the fact that it is light
green in colour.
(See *Sapsago*.)

KUMINOST

A type of spiced cheese produced in many of
the Scandinavian countries. Cumin and caraway seeds are used to flavour the curd. Among

Kasseri (left), Kashkaval (top), Kefalotyri (right)

the many types is a variety made from skimmed milk which has a low fat content. (See *Friesian*, *Leyden* and *Nokkelost*.)

LA BOUILLE

A Brie/Camembert style French double crème cheese. The cheese has a bloomy white rind with reddish pigmentation. The cheese is similar to the French cheese Monsieur but is matured for a longer period (up to three months). With a fat content of 60 per cent the cheese has a richer, fuller Brie flavour. (See *Monsieur* and *Double Crèmes*.)

LA GRAPPE

This is a popular French processed cheese distinguished by the fact that grape skins and pips form its rind. In the USA this cheese is known simply as Grappe and has a wax coating. (See *Processed Cheese*.)

LA VACHE QUI RIT

A well-known brand name for a French range of processed Gruyère. (See *Processed Cheese*.)

LANCASHIRE

Country of origin: Great Britain (England).

Background: 'Many's the night I've dreamed of cheese—toasted mostly,' sighed Ben Gunn in Stevenson's *Treasure Island*. Poor Gunn was probably thinking of Lancashire, England's most illustrious toasting cheese. Indeed, it was once known as Leigh Toaster from the small town in the Fylde where it was made, between the Ribble and Lune rivers, eleven miles from Manchester.

Description: Lancashire is a white buttery cheese with a clean and mild taste which strengthens the longer the cheese ages. The cheese can be made in cylindrical shapes weighing about 18 kg (40 lb) or in rindless blocks. It is also marketed in small vacuum-packed pieces.

Lancashire has a softer texture than Cheddar and is rather more moist. After maturing for two months it is softly ripe. Melted, it turns into a succulent, creamy mass and poured like rich cream and grilled until a little colour appears, it has no rival.

An interesting variation, Lancashire Sage, has fresh sage leaves added to it when it is made.

Wines: Fruity reds; beer; the English also recommend it with medium sherry or madeira. Serve: The best cheese in the world to use for Welsh rarebit; it also goes well with biscuits, and is suitable for topping soups. Fat content: 45 per cent. Type: Cheddar family. Aroma: Unpronounced.

LAPLAND

The Laplanders make this cheese from reindeer's milk in an unusual dumbbell-like shape. The cheese itself is very hard, Swiss-like.

LARRON

A version of Maroilles—a strong smelling and gamy, pungent tasting French washed rind cheese. (See *Maroilles*.)

LAUGHING COW

A famous range of French processed cheese. (See *Processed Cheese*.)

Lancashire (centre), Leicester (below)

LEICESTER

Country of origin: Great Britain (England).

Background: This used to be one of England's most popular cheeses until it fell out of favour at the end of the 1930s. In recent years Leicester has made a comeback but not to the extent of being classed as the second best cheese in England—a position it once held.

Description: Leicester is a rich deep orange coloured cheese that looks particularly striking on a cheese board. It gets its colouring from the use of an annatto dye, like Cheshire and Double Gloucester. Leicester is matured for a minimum period of ten to twelve weeks. The cheese has a higher moisture content than Cheddar, which means a shorter life span and a softer body. Fully ripe at six months, it is past its prime at one year. It is a loose-textured cheese, rather flaky, with a clean-tasting, creamy, mellow flavour which could be described as medium-strong. The cheese leaves a lingering rich mellow aftertaste on the palate.

Like the other traditional English cheeses it is made in large cylindrical shapes weighing up to 20 kg (45 lb) and is also marketed in rindless blocks or small vacuum-packed pieces. Leicester melts quickly, making it good for toasting.

Wines: Light red wines; beer and cider.
Serve: End of meals, in sandwiches; a good snack cheese; try it with spring onions.
Fat content: 45 per cent.
Type: Cheddar family.
Aroma: Unpronounced.

L'EXPLORATEUR

A French triple crème cheese made in cylinder shapes some 5 cm (2 in) high and 7.5 cm (3 in) in diameter. The cheese is ripened for three weeks during which it develops a delicate, white bloomy rind. Its interior paste is thick, rich and creamy—a texture that is more than matched by its luxurious flavour. The cheese has a 75 per cent fat content.
(See *Triple Crèmes*.)

LEYDEN

Country of origin: Holland.

Background: A traditional spiced cheese formerly produced on farms in the north-western area of the Zuid Holland province. The cheese is stamped with two crossed keys, the symbol of the university city of Leyden.

Description: Leyden is a firm-textured cheese with a semi-hard dark-yellow rind covered with red wax. The cheese is flavoured with caraway and cumin seeds which are scattered through its light yellow interior paste. Leyden is made in cylindrical shapes approximately 40 cm (16 in) in diameter and some 7.5 cm (3 in) thick. Such cheeses can weigh up to 10 kg (22 lb). In taste Leyden is tangy and spicy, nutty and tasty—one of the better spiced cheeses. Two versions are made; one from whole cow's milk and one from skimmed cow's milk. This factor affects the fat content of the cheese.

Nokkelost is the Norwegian version of Leyden (*nokkelost* means 'key' cheese). It is made in cylindrical shapes or rectangular blocks. Although a copy, it tastes quite unlike Leyden. As well as being spiced with caraway and cumin seeds, cloves are also added. It is milder than Leyden, spicy but rather sweeter, softer and more buttery.

Wines: Leyden, fruity red wines, dry whites; the Dutch recommend it with gin; Nokkelost would go with a medium sherry, blanquette, semillon or white burgundies.
Serve: Good sandwich and snack cheeses blending well with tomatoes, cucumber and lettuce; end of meals.
Fat content: 20-40 per cent.
Type: Spiced.
Aroma: Leyden is noticeably spicy; Nokkelost smells of cloves.

LIEDERKRANZ

Country of origin: USA.

Background: Liederkranz came into being towards the end of last century when a New

York cheesemaker attempted to copy a popular German cheese called Bismark Schlosskäse. He succeeded in creating Liederkranz—a cheese with a character entirely of its own and one of the few cheeses considered to be genuine American originals. Liederkranz takes its name from a German singing society to which the cheesemaker belonged; it means 'wreath of song'.

Description: Liederkranz is made in small oblong loaves weighing around 120 g (4 oz). It is a soft, surface-ripened cheese made from cow's milk which is matured for three to four weeks. The cheese has a thin, light orange rind and pale yellow interior, very soft and spreadable and of an almost honey-like consistency when ripe. It has a full and pungent aroma but despite this in taste it is not as strong as one might expect—full flavoured and pungent but rather delicate, rich and distinctive at the same time.

Liederkranz comes foil-wrapped and does not have a long life. It is important to get the cheese at its peak before it becomes over-aged.

Wines: Goes extremely well with beer.
Serve: At end of meals; as a snack on dark bread with beer.
Fat content: 50 per cent.
Type: Strong smelling monastery style.
Aroma: Full and distinctive.

LIMBURGER

Country of origin: Belgium.

Background: This cheese is made in several European countries and is so popular in Germany that it is often thought to have originated there. In fact it was first produced in the Middle Ages by monks in the province of Limburg in Belgium. It is one of the world's most famous 'smelly' cheeses.

Description: Limburger is made from cow's milk, usually in rectangular shapes 15 cm (6 in) long by 7.5 cm (3 in) wide and high. Smaller cube-shaped sizes are also made. The cheese is semi-soft, supple feeling with the smooth, thin, reddish to brownish rind which is a feature of this type of washed rind cheese.

Limburger is surface ripened in a humid atmosphere for three months and has a smooth-textured yellow interior with a few holes, small and irregular in size. The cheese is usually marketed wrapped in foil.

Limburger is distinguished by its powerful odour, very strong and rank—and for many people quite overpowering. Its taste is not as bad (or as good, depending on your point of view) as its smell, but it is still a memorably tangy, pungent and gamy tasting cheese.

American Limburger is usually somewhat milder than the European varieties, which can also tend to get a trifle over-ripe by the time they reach their overseas destination—enhancing their strength even further.

Wines: Full-bodied reds; in Germany it is often eaten with beer.
Serve: As a snack on dark breads with strong-flavoured vegetables like onions, radishes and shallots.
Fat content: 30-40 per cent.
Type: Strong smelling/monastery.
Aroma: Pronounced.

LIPTAUER

A Hungarian cheese from the Province of Liptow, from which the cheese takes its name. It is an unusual cheese in that it is designed to be eaten with a variety of flavouring agents throughout its body; these include paprika, capers, chives, garlic, onions, hot peppers or finely chopped olives. The cheese itself, made from sheep's milk, is soft, faintly oily and has the familiar granular, gritty sheep's milk cheese texture. It is not a particularly strong cheese; the ingredients used to flavour it provide its appeal—a sort of cheese-type smorgasbord.

LIVAROT

Country of origin: France.

Background: An old Normandy cheese noted for both strong taste and strong smell. Versions

Liederkranz (photo courtesy Borden Foods)

of this type of cheese have been made in Normandy since the thirteenth century.

Description: Livarot is a soft, washed rind cheese, surface ripened in humid cellars for three months to allow full bacterial development. It is made from cow's milk in the shape of small discs up to 12.5 cm (5 in) in diameter and 5 cm (2 in) thick.

Like all cheeses of this kind, its rind is smooth, with a glossy finish which varies in colour from reddish-brown to dark brown. The interior paste is cream yellow; when fully ripe Livarot is soft textured to the point when it could almost be spread. After manufacture the cheese is wrapped around with a band of five reeds. It was this practice that caused it to be known as a 'Five-Striper' or 'Livarot-Colonel' in France.

The military reference is quite apt; there is nothing half-hearted about a Livarot. The cheese has a highly developed taste, very strong, spicy and tangy, and well-matched by its powerful odour, which many people find somewhat overpowering.

Wines: Strong, full-bodied reds, port or sherry.
Serve: End of meals; snacks.
Fat content: 40-45 per cent.
Type: Monastery/strong smelling.
Aroma: Pronounced.

LOAF

This is simply the name given to several types of cheese that are made in a rectangular loaf shape. Formerly, most cheeses of this type were processed, but there has been an increasing trend to make more and more natural cheeses ranging from Cheddar to Emmental in rindless rectangular blocks.

LODIGIANO

An Italian grating cheese of the Grana style. The most famous cheese of this type is Parmesan.
(See *Grana* and *Parmesan.*)

LOMBARDO

A Grana style Italian grating cheese, sometimes also called Lombardy. The best known cheese of this type is Parmesan.
(See *Grana* and *Parmesan.*)

LONGHORN

An American Cheddar so called because of its tall conical shape. Its flavour varies from mild to robust depending on age.
(See *Cheddar.*)

LUCULLUS

A French triple crème cheese made in the shape of a small cylinder 7.5 cm (3 in) in diameter and 5 cm (2 in) high. A soft textured cheese with a light bloomy surface rind, slightly pink in colour. Lucullus is a thickly rich creamy cheese with a lightly nutty flavour. It has a fat content of 75 per cent.
(See *Triple Crèmes.*)

MACONNAIS

A square shaped French goat's milk cheese.
(See *Chèvres.*)

MACROBERTSON

(See Australian *Cheddars.*)

MAGNUM

A French double crème cheese which is ripened for a three week period and develops a light bloomy rind. The interior is rich, luscious and creamy. The cheese has a 72 per cent fat content.
(See *Double Crèmes.*)

MAINLAND

(See New Zealand *Cheddars*.)

MAINZ

Country of origin: Germany.

Background: A member of the family of German skimmed sour milk cheeses. It takes its name from an important port on the Rhine. Mainz is related to Harz cheese. Both have a high protein content and a low fat content and are noted for their powerful flavour and aroma.

Description: This cheese is essentially the same as Harz. It is made in small, rubbery discs about 5 cm (2 in) in diameter and 2.5 cm (1 in) thick. The smooth surface may be golden yellow to reddish-brown; the interior is a pale glassy yellow.

These little cheeses possess a very pungent taste and odour and while they range in degree of sharpness of flavour even the milder versions would be found extremely potent by the uninitiated.

Wines: Often eaten with beer; sometimes with cider.
Serve: Snacks.
Fat content: Less than 10 per cent.
Type: Strong smelling.
Aroma: Pronounced.
(See *Harz* and *Sour Curd Cheeses*.)

MALAKOFF

A small, soft, bloomy rind cream cheese which weighs between 100 g and 250 g (4-8 oz). The cheese is essentially a version of the more famous Neufchâtel, considered one of the oldest of the Normandy cheeses.
(See *Neufchâtel*.)

MANCHEGO

Country of origin: Spain.

Description: This is Spain's most popular

and one of its oldest cheeses. It is made from sheep's milk in large cylinder shapes and is matured for about one month. The cheese has a hard yellow natural rind with a firmish textured interior paste varying in colour from white to yellow, sometimes with, sometimes without holes.

At its best an excellent sheep's milk cheese, full flavoured and rich tasting with a distinctive 'sheepy' tang.

Wines: Fruity reds.
Serve: End of meals; snacks.
Fat content: 57 per cent.
Type: Sheep's milk.
Aroma: Noticeable sheepy aroma.

MANTECA

An unusual pasta filata style Italian cheese that is made and looks like a small, rounded Caciocavallo but has in its heart a knob of butter (usually sweet whey butter). Cut open, the Manteca presents a striking combination of texture and colour: the outer part of the cheese, usually smoked, being yellow-brown, while the egg of butter within is a straw yellow colour. This cheese is also known as Burrino. It has a mild, sweet buttery flavour.
(See *Burrino*.)

MAORI GOUDA

This New Zealand cheese tastes quite different to the famous Dutch cheese on which it is based. Maori Gouda is a strong yellow in colour; while initially bland tasting it has a pronounced aftertaste that is reminiscent of sour milk, almost tobacco-like.
(See *Gouda*.)

MARGOTIN

A French double crème cheese available with a covering of pepper or flavoured with herbs. A

cheese with a 60 per cent fat content—rich, creamy and tangy.
(See *Double Crèmes*.)

MARIBO

Country of origin: Denmark.

Background: Maribo is another member of the numerous Danish Samsoe family.

Description: Maribo is a golden wheel-shaped cheese with rounded sides and edges, measuring 43 cm (17 in) in diameter. Whole cheeses weigh in the region of 13 kg (30 lb).

The cheese has a thin, dry, yellow rind and a rich yellow interior, compact and firm-textured with a large number of small, irregular, rice-sized holes spread across it. The holes are quite close together and uniformly spaced.

Maribo undergoes three to four months' maturing which results in a clean taste, bland and mild but just faintly acidulous; it has a noticeable aftertaste, rather like a lighter flavoured Havarti. Aged versions can develop a bitter-sweet aftertaste.

Versions of this cheese, which is made from cow's milk, are also made in rectangular shapes, with or without rinds.

Wines: Light dry whites; medium strength reds, rosés.
Serve: An all-purpose Danish table cheese; goes well with vegetables such as radishes, tomatoes, green peppers and celery.
Fat content: 45 per cent.
Type: Bland/buttery.
Aroma: Unpronounced.

MAROILLES

Country of origin: France.

Background: This cheese was developed by monks at the monastery of Maroilles in the tenth century. The French refer to it as Vieux Puant—Old Stinker.

Description: Maroilles is a soft, washed-rind cheese, powerful in both aroma and flavour. It is made in squares of about 12.5 cm (5 in),

and 7.5 cm (3 in) thick. The reddish-brown rind is smooth and shiny, the result of the continual washings the cheese receives during its curing process. The yellow interior paste is semi-firm and supple; when ripe quite soft. During its four month ripening period, the cheese is regularly brushed and bathed in beer.

Maroilles is one of the best-known French 'smelly' cheeses, with an extremely strong bouquet and gamy, tangy, potent flavour. It is made in several shapes and sizes, versions of it being known as Quart, Larron, Boulette, Dauphin and Sorbais.

Wines: Strong, full-bodied reds.
Serve: End of meals with crusty bread; snacks.
Fat content: 45-50 per cent.
Type: Monastery/strong smelling.
Aroma: Pronounced.

MASCARPONE

Country of origin: Italy.

Background: Originally from Lombardy, now made all over Italy, Mascarpone is made from fresh cream, usually in the winter months.

Description: In appearance Mascarpone resembles clotted cream, and appears as a soft white mass usually packaged in plastic tubs and containers. It is a cheese with a high fat content and some authorities challenge whether it should be considered a cheese or a cream. At any rate, all find it delectable—very soft, rich, creamy and buttery in flavour, somewhat like whipped cream, in fact. In Italy it is often sold in muslin bags with sweetened fruits.

When aged Mascarpone develops a firmer texture and a buttery colour and is used for grating.

Wines: Light whites of the style of moselle, traminer and auslese, or a delicate sweet moscato wine.
Serve: Usually eaten as a dessert with sugar and fruit; goes excellently with fruit as varied as strawberries and watermelon. Sometimes mixed with brandy or liqueurs.
Fat content: 60 per cent.
Type: Unripened double crème.
Aroma: Unpronounced.

MATURE EDAM

A Dutch Edam cheese which has been matured for up to one year (Edams are normally matured for between three and four months). Mature Edam is therefore a much stronger tasting cheese—harder and drier and slightly more salty in flavour.
(See *Edam*.)

MATURE GOUDA

A version of Dutch Gouda that has been matured for up to a year. This makes a much stronger tasting cheese with a pronounced and distinctive aftertaste. The rind is a darker yellow than with normal Goudas which are matured for between three and four months.
(See *Gouda*.)

MEJETTE

A whey, Cottage style cheese, the best known version of which is Ricotta.
(See *Ricotta*.)

MIDDEBARE

This is simply the name of the largest sized Edam that the Dutch produce. The cheese can weigh up to 6 kg (14 lb).
(See *Edam*.)

MILANO

A stracchino type Italian cheese sometimes called Stracchino di Milano. Milano is a soft, fast ripening (it is left to mature for only 20 days) table cheese made in Lombardy; mild, sweet and rich tasting—a stracchino *dolce*

rather than *piccante*. It can be compared to Bel Paese and Crescenza.
(See *Stracchino* and *Bel Paese*.)

MILKANA

Brand name for a processed Emmentaler cheese range.
(See *Processed Cheese*.)

MIMOLETTE

Country of origin: Holland.

Background: This cheese is widely made in France and though often considered French, is in fact Dutch, and related to Edam and Gouda.

Description: Mimolette is a particularly striking and attractive cheese. Made in a spherical shape about 17.5 cm (7 in) in diameter and 12.5 cm (5 in) high, it is coloured a bright, glowing orange by the use of annatto dye. The cheese has a wax-covered, thin, natural rind and a firm, supple-textured interior usually free of holes.
  Mimolette is cured for a minimum period of six months and is made from cow's milk. It is a clean, uncomplicated cheese tasting slightly nutty, rather salty—something like a mature Gouda in flavour and texture.
  French Mimolette is similar but rather softer in texture and creamier.

Wines: Light reds; rosés; beer.
Serve: A tasty snack and sandwich cheese; its colour makes it look striking on a cheese board.
Fat content: 45 per cent.
Type: Bland/buttery.
Aroma: Unpronounced.

MINI ESROM

A small-sized version of the Danish cheese Esrom. The mini version is made in a rectangular brick shape weighing between 250 g and 500 g ($\frac{1}{2}$-1 lb).
(See *Esrom*.)

MINI FYNBO

A smaller sized version of the Danish cheese Fynbo. Mini Fynbo is made in 250 g (½ lb) sizes.
(See *Fynbo*.)

MITZITHRA

A Greek cheese made from the surplus whey left over when making Feta. Fresh sheep's milk is added to the whey and the two are mixed and curdled. After the whey has been removed the curd is drained and pressed and sold fresh and unripened. The cheese is also known as Pot Cheese—a type of Greek cottage cheese.

MOE

This is one of the two Camembert-style cheeses made in Australia. Moe, also known as Mountain Boy, comes from Victoria. The other Australian Camembert is Riviana from New South Wales.
(See *Camembert*.)

MOLBO

Country of origin: Denmark.

Background: Molbo is a Danish version of the Dutch cheese Edam, and was once known as Danish Edam.

Description: Molbo is a ball-shaped cheese with a small flat area top and bottom, which weighs approximately 2-3 kg (4-6 lb). The cheese has a dry, yellowish rind, red-waxed and a bright yellow to white interior. Its texture is firm and supple and contains a few regularly shaped holes—pea-sized or smaller. In flavour it is mild, bland, buttery, just slightly salty with a slightly acid aftertaste. Molbo is made from cow's milk.

Wines: Beaujolais-style reds, light dry whites.
Serve: End of meals, snacks; the cheese slices well, making it good for sandwiches; its bland-

ness makes it suitable for children. Molbo goes with vegetables such as radishes, green peppers and grated carrots.
Fat content: 45 per cent (minimum).
Type: Bland/buttery.
Aroma: Unpronounced.

MONCENISIO

This is an Italian blue vein cheese similar to Gorgonzola.
(See *Gorgonzola*.)

MON CHOU

A Dutch double crème cheese with a 73 per cent fat content made in 100 g (3½ oz) packs wrapped in aluminium foil. Soft, very rich and creamy with a faintly acid tinge.
(See *Double Crèmes*.)

MONSEER

Country of origin: Germany.

Description: Monseer is a washed rind, monastery style cheese made from cow's milk. It has a thin, reddish-yellow rind. The cheese's interior is semi-soft, supple feeling, yellow in colour and dotted with a few irregular shaped holes. The cheeses are made in small wheel shapes about 15 cm (6 in) in diameter by 5 cm (2 in) thick; they weigh about 1 kg (2¼ lb). Smaller versions are also marketed.

The cheese has a full, distinctive, lingering taste, earthy and appealing, sharpish but not overstrong; somewhere between Esrom and Munster. It has also been compared to a mild Limburger.

Wines: Goes with reds and also a good cheese to eat with beer.
Serve: Good snack-type cheese.
Fat content: 50 per cent.
Type: Monastery.
Aroma: Noticeable but not overpronounced.

MONSIEUR

Country of origin: France.

Background: This is a Normandy cheese developed towards the end of last century by a farmer named, appropriately enough, Fromage (cheese). Consequently it is sometimes known as Monsieur Fromage.

Description: Monsieur is a soft cheese with a bloomy rind, like Camembert and Brie, 7.5 cm (3 in) in diameter and about 5 cm (2 in) thick. It is made from cow's milk in a method similar to Brie, but is enriched with cream and has a higher fat content. The cheese has a downy white rind dotted with red pigments, a fresh, pleasant aroma and a rich, fruity, pronounced creamy flavour. It can be considered a richer, creamier, fuller Brie-style cheese. At its peak condition, it is highly regarded.

Wines: Full-bodied burgundy-style reds.
Serve: End of meals.
Fat content: 60 per cent.
Type: Matured double crème/Brie/Camembert.
Aroma: Unpronounced.

MONTASIO

A hard Italian cheese made in the Swiss style and similar to the more famous Fontina. Fully matured versions of this cheese are used for grating.
(See *Fontina*.)

MONTEREY JACK

Country of origin: USA.

Background: A Cheddar-style cheese originally from Monterey County, California, believed to have first been made in 1892. It is still made in California but also in other parts of America such as Wisconsin.

Description: The cheese is made in loaf and also wheel shapes. The largest size would be in the region of 18 kg (40 lb) but smaller sizes are made. There are two varieties, one made from whole cow's milk and one from skimmed milk. Monterey Jack is more white than yellow as the cheese is not treated with a colouring additive. It has a thin natural rind (it can also be obtained in rindless blocks) and a supple, resilient texture. The cheese is matured for only between three and six weeks which puts it at the very mild end of the Cheddar taste scale. One variety is aged for six months and is used for grating.

Wines: Light reds; dry whites.
Serve: As a snack; goes reasonably well with most vegetables and fruit.
Fat content: 50 per cent.
Type: Cheddar.
Aroma: Unpronounced.

MONTHERY

A Brie type French cheese made in two sizes: the larger one has a 35 cm (14 in) diameter and weighs about 2 kg (5 lb); the smaller weighs about 1¼ kg (3 lb).
(See *Brie*.)

MONTRACHET

Country of origin: France.

Background: This semi-fresh (it can be matured for as little as a week) goat's milk cheese from Burgundy takes its name from the famous white wine associated with the area. It is also known as Chèvre du Montrachet.

Description: Montrachet is made in 10 cm (4 in) tall cylinder shapes about 5 cm (2 in) in diameter. This is a soft, moist, pure white cheese with scarcely any discernible rind and a texture close to cottage cheese. The cheese is one of the best examples of the mild, fresh French chèvres—at its best light and delectable but still distinctively 'goaty'. It is usually packed in chestnut or grape leaves in containers; some versions are ash covered. Besides the standard log shape, it is also made in a creamier version packaged in 200 g (6 oz) plastic cups.

Wines: Light and fruity reds; light whites.
Serve: End of meals.
Fat content: 45 per cent.
Type: Goat's milk.
Aroma: Unpronounced.

MORBIER

Country of origin: France.

Description: This is a monastery style cheese made in the shape of a thick disc up to 40 cm (16 in) in diameter and 10 cm (4 in) thick. The cheese has a light grey rind and a very distinctive interior—ivory white with a black streak running horizontally through the middle. Morbier, named after the village of Morbier in Champagne, is made from cow's milk and is matured for between two and three months.

It is a pressed, uncooked cheese, firm textured but with a certain suppleness. Older versions of this cheese develop a pronounced and distinctive tang; young ones are essentially mild and bland.

Wines: Any light but fruity red wine.
Serve: An interesting cheese for the cheese board at the end of a meal; well suited for snacks.
Fat content: 45 per cent.
Type: Monastery.
Aroma: Unpronounced.

MOTHAIS

A French chèvre or goat's milk cheese.
(See *Chèvres*.)

MOZZARELLA

Country of origin: Italy.

Background: This cheese, widely used in cooking, belongs to the drawn curd (*pasta filata*) family of Italian cheeses. It was formerly made only from buffalo's milk but is now also made from cow's milk.

Description: Mozzarella is an unripened pasta filata cheese. In Italy (as with some types made in America), it is sold when it is only two to three days old. The cheese, made in various shapes—spherical, oval, rectangular, pear-shaped—is pure white with a soft plastic body, rather moist, and has a smooth close texture. In flavour it is mild, delicate, creamy, vaguely sweet.

Mozzarella's freshness can be determined by its colouring (always white, never yellow) and its firmness to the touch. The cheese should be used within a few days of purchase as it does not have a long life. Related cheeses include Treccia and Scarmorza.

Wines: Light whites or rosés.
Serve: Because of its elastic character and mild flavour it is widely used as a cooking cheese—melted over hamburgers, pizzas, toasted sandwiches or as a cheesy layer in lasagne-type dishes.
Fat content: 40-45 per cent.
Type: Fresh, unripened.
Aroma: Unpronounced.

MUNSTER

Country of origin: France.

Background: This cheese, which comes from the province of Alsace, is thought of as the region's 'national' cheese. It was developed in the Middle Ages in the Vosges Mountains close to the German border. Münster is extremely popular in Germany and much is produced there.

Description: Münster is usually made in large disc shapes measuring up to 20 cm (8 in) in diameter and 5 cm (2 in) thick. It is a washed-rind, surface-ripened cheese, one of the most famous of its kind in the world. The cheese has a smooth, reddish-coloured outer rind and a semi-soft interior paste, a rich straw yellow in colour, sometimes dotted with a few small, irregular-shaped holes. The larger sized cheeses may be ripened in atmospheres containing a high degree of humidity for up to three months. Smaller cheeses—Münster is also made in disc shapes measuring only 10 cm (4 in)

Varieties of Mozzarella

in diameter—may undergo a shorter ripening period of six weeks.

The bacterial development on the surface of the cheese gives Münster a distinctive, powerful and penetrating aroma. Like its taste, the aroma varies with the maturity of the cheese but is always noticeably distinctive. Münster is a strong tasting cheese, tangy, spicy and full-flavoured. It can get rank when over-ripe.

German Münster is as pungent a cheese as the French but Mynster, a Danish variety, and American Muenster are very different. Both are mild and bland (the Danish version, which tastes like a mild Port Salut, has a higher fat content than the American and tends to be creamier), undemanding and innocuous compared to the full-blooded robustness of the French and German cheeses and despite the similarity of names should not be confused with them.

Wines: Well-aged reds of high calibre.
Serve: End of meals; as a snack.
Fat content: 45 per cent.
Type: Strong smelling/monastery.
Aroma: Pronounced.

MYCELLA

Country of origin: Denmark.

Background: One of the best-known of Denmark's blue-veined cheeses, sold on a world market. Mycella was once known as Danish Gorgonzola and in fact is closely modelled on the famous Italian cheese.

Description: Mycella is a tall, cylindrical-shaped cheese measuring approximately 14 cm (6 in) in height and approximately 23 cm (9 in) in diameter. The weight can range between 5-9 kg (11-20 lb), full size. Smaller pieces are sold in 125 g (4 oz) and 250 g (8 oz) packets, wrapped in aluminium foil.

The cheese has a dry, slightly greasy rind, white to brown in colour, with a soft, white to cream interior. It is marbled throughout with evenly-spaced blue-green veins, the result of inoculation with the *Penicillium* spore. Mycella has a soft body and a rich, creamy flavour—less salty than many other blue-veined cheeses

—and is mildly aromatic rather than sharp or noticeably salty in taste.

Wines: Any strong, full-bodied red wine.
Serve: End of meal as a dessert cheese; as a salad dressing; as an hors d'oeuvre on a cocktail stick with green grapes or fresh strawberries.
Fat content: 50 per cent (minimum).
Type: Blue vein.
Aroma: Unpronounced, slight mould smell.

MYNSTER

Country of origin: Denmark.

Background: This is a Danish version of the French cheese Münster, but a much milder and less dramatic version. It is so different, in fact, from the French cheese that the two should not be compared.

Description: A flat round cheese measuring 25 cm (10 in) in diameter and 7 cm (3 in) in height, Mynster has a dry yellowish rind and a yellow to white interior which contains a few round holes. Its texture is firm and supple and the cheese has a mild, creamy flavour far less pronounced in taste and smell than the French original.

Wines: Light red and rosé wines, dry whites.
Serve: End of meals; light snacks; the cheese slices easily and is suitable for sandwiches.
Fat content: 50 per cent.
Type: Bland/buttery.
Aroma: Unpronounced.

MYSOST

This is a version of the Norwegian whey cheese Gjetöst made entirely from cow's milk. (See *Gjetöst*.)

NANTAIS

Country of origin: France.

Background: Also known as Curé Nantais and Fromage du Curé (Priest's Cheese) as it was developed by a parish priest late last century.

Description: This is a washed rind cheese with a yellow to orange coloured, smooth rind; the cheese is supple and resilient feeling but has a softer, rather moist, yellow interior. Nantais is made in a square shape with rounded corners measuring about 8 cm (3 in) square and approximately 5 cm (2 in) thick. Made from cow's milk, it is ripened in humid cellars for one month. It is a monastery style cheese but a strong, full flavoured one; pronouncedly earthy and penetrating on the palate.

Wines: Full flavoured reds and dry whites.
Serve: End of meals with French bread.
Fat content: 40 per cent.
Type: Monastery.
Aroma: Full and distinctive.

NEC PLUS EXTRA

A French range of processed cheese.
(See *Processed Cheese.*)

NEUFCHATEL

Country of origin: France.

Background: This cheese comes from northern Normandy, a renowned milk-producing area. Neufchâtel has been made there for centuries and is considered one of the oldest of the Normandy cheeses.

Description: Neufchâtel is the best-known of a number of French bloomy-rind cheeses characterised by white, downy or velvety surface moulds, small sizes and soft, creamy textures. In taste these cheeses are essentially mild but rich, delectable and just slightly salty.
    They come in a variety of shapes—cylindrical, tube-shaped, square, even heart-shaped —but all are small, usually weighing no more than between 100 g to 250 g (4-8 oz).
    Neufchâtel is cured for a period of three weeks, during which time a fluffy white mould, tinged with a reddish pigmentation, appears on its surface. Other cheeses of this type include Malakoff, Gournay, Bondon, Briquette and Coeur, which differ from Neufchâtel only in their shape and size.

It is important to buy this type of cheese when it is fresh—excessive saltiness or dryness are signs of an over-aged cheese—and then they should be eaten as soon as possible. All such cheeses are made from cow's milk.

Wines: Serve with delicate wines with a fruity character. Whites—traminer, white hermitage, pinot, sauternes, champagne, rheingau white; reds—tawny port, cabernet shiraz; will also go quite adequately with tea or coffee.
Serve: Ideal for dessert or mid-morning snack; at end of meals with thin table wafer biscuits; with a granular pear and crusty bread; if the cheese is old and dry, grate a little into an omelette.
Fat content: 45 per cent.
Type: Mild (cream cheese).
Aroma: Unpronounced.

NEW ZEALAND BLUE

A dry, rather salty blue vein, quite sharp and pronounced in flavour.
(See *Blue Veins.*)

NOKKELOST

This is a Norwegian version of the Dutch spiced cheese Leyden. Nokkelost is made in cylindrical shapes and rectangular blocks and is spiced with cloves. It is sweeter, softer and more buttery than Leyden.
(See *Leyden.*)

NORWEGIAN BLUE

Country of origin: Norway.

Description: This is Norway's contribution to blue veins, a semi-soft cheese, matured for two to three months. It is made in large cylinder shapes and also sold in foil-wrapped wedges. The cheese has greenish-blue veining and a pliable, creamy but sometimes slightly crumbly texture. Norwegian Blue is a copy of Roquefort although it is made from cow's not sheep's milk. A well balanced blue-veined cheese, piquant and distinctive, interesting and complex in taste—well regarded.

Wines: Full-bodied reds.
Serve: End of meals; the Norwegians recommend it on bread and butter covered with chopped radishes, topped off with canned fruit, parsley and lettuce.
Fat content: 45 per cent.
Type: Blue vein.
Aroma: Light mould smell.

NORWEGIAN EDAM

A close model of the traditional Dutch cheese. It has a slightly acid flavour but is very buttery with a sprinkling of small even holes throughout. Yellow in colour.
(See *Edam.*)

NORWEGIAN EMMENTALER

A sweeter, more watery version of the famous Swiss cheese, not so recognisably nutty in flavour.
(See *Emmentaler.*)

NORWEGIAN SAINT PAULIN

Originally modelled on the famous French cheese, this is creamy soft, pliable in texture, rather plastic, quite mild.
(See *Port Salut* and *Saint Paulin.*)

OKA

Country of origin: Canada.

Background: Oka cheese was developed by the Trappist monks at Oka in Quebec.

Description: In shape, style and size Oka is very similar to Port Salut and Saint Paulin. However, it is considered a very fine example of this style of cheese—rich, creamy, tangy and distinctive.

Wines: Full-bodied beaujolais-style wines.
Serve: End of meals.
Fat content: 45-50 per cent.
Type: Monastery.
Aroma: Unpronounced.
(See *Port Salut* and *Saint Paulin.*)

OKATO MATURED

A New Zealand Cheddar and, as the name suggests, a well matured one—a good, fulsome, strong tasting cheese.
(See *Cheddar.*)

OLIVET

This is a soft, bloomy rind cheese from the Orléans area of France. There are two kinds: Olivet Bleu which has a bluish surface mould and Olivet Cendré which is coated with and matured in ashes. Both are Camembert type cheese, Olivet Cendré being the stronger flavoured of the two. Rarely seen outside of France.
(See *Camembert.*)

OLMUTZER QUARGEL

This is a Bavarian cheese which is a member of the German family of sour curd cheeses. These cheeses are noted for their low fat content, high protein value, aroma and penetrating flavour. Olmützer Quargel is a particularly strong version of this type of cheese.
(See *Sour Curd Cheeses*, *Harz* and *Mainz.*)

PANEDDA

An Italian pasta filata (drawn curd) style cheese. The more famous cheeses of this type are Caciocavallo and Provolone, widely used in cooking for lasagne-type dishes.
(See *Pasta Filata* and *Provolone.*)

PANNERONE

Country of origin: Italy.

Background: This is a stracchino cheese closely related to Gorgonzola.

Description: The full name of this cheese in Italian is Stracchino di Gorgonzola bianco or Gorgonzola dolce. It is called White Gorgonzola because it is ripened for no longer than one month and does not take on the greenish-blue veining of its famous relative.

Apart from this important point the cheese is made in a similar fashion to Gorgonzola. In appearance it is flat, rectangular in shape, yellow in colour with a series of small holes set closely together. The cheeses can weigh up to about 10 kg (22 lb). Pannerone is milder than Gorgonzola, lacking the latter's pungency, but with a certain tang or middling sharpness to its taste.

Wines: Full-bodied reds.
Serve: End of meals.
Fat content: 48 per cent.
Type: Bland/buttery.
Aroma: Unpronounced.

PARMESAN

Country of origin: Italy.

Background: This is the best-known of Italy's large range of Grana cheeses, so-called because of their granular texture, which have been made in Italy since the thirteenth century. Other cheeses, which are often marketed under the name Parmesan outside Italy, include Lodigiano, Lombardo, Veneto, Bresciano, Grana Padano and Emiliano. Parmesan's correct name is Parmigiano Reggiano and it was first made in the area of Parma.

Description: Parmesan is the world's most famous grating cheese, used to complement and flavour a great variety of dishes. It is made in large cylindrical wheels up to 45 cm (18 in) in diameter and 23 cm (9 in) thick. The cheese is straw yellow in colour with a hard, brownish rind often coated with a blackish protective mixture of oil and umber.

The cheeses can spend up to three years maturing, which gives them a very hard but brittle and flaky texture making them ideal for grating. Due to its hard texture and low moisture content, the cheese will keep almost indefinitely. In flavour Parmesan is sharp, piquant and distinctive. An official Italian publication on the subject describes the cheese as having a 'fragrant, delicate taste but not spicy' and 'melting in the mouth when eaten'.

Australian Parmesan undergoes a minimum maturing period of one year but this is often extended up to two. It is made in 13 kg (29 lb) cylindrical forms and at least one company markets the cheese with the traditional waxy black surface coating. It is also available in wedges and in grated form, but all Parmesans are at their best when freshly grated.

American Parmesan is made chiefly in Wisconsin and Michigan and is matured for a minimum of fourteen months.

Wines: Full-bodied reds such as Chianti.
Serve: Parmesan's piquant flavour complements many dishes, including savoury sauces and omelettes. Mixed with fresh unripened cheeses such as Ricotta, it can be used as a filling for ravioli and cannelloni dishes. It can be sprinkled over pizzas and soups such as minestrone and used with buttered noodles, spaghetti and rice.
Fat content: 32-35 per cent.
Type: Extra-hard grating cheese.
Aroma: Unpronounced.

PASTA FILATA

The name refers not to a cheese but to a range of Italian cheeses which have their curds placed in hot water after the whey has been drained off. While the curd is in a plastic and malleable condition, it is drawn out and stretched and manipulated into shape by hand. Aged cheeses of this type can be used for grating. Examples include Caciocavallo and Provolone. Other types, such as Mozzarella and Scarmorza, are not ripened and are softer in texture and rather moist. They are often used in cooking, particularly for pizzas.
(See *Caciocavallo, Provolone, Mozzarella*.)

PASTORELLO

Country of origin: Australia.

Background: One of the few cheeses unique to Australia, Pastorello was developed in Sydney under the direction of Italian born Dr Daniele Lostia. Though it has been likened to France's Fontal, Dr Lostia is adamant that the cheese is an original.

Description: Pastorello is a fairly soft cheese with a relatively high moisture content. Though fairly bland in flavour it develops gradually to mellow over its life-span of up to six months. Its appearance is interesting as the freshly made curd is drained in baskets so that a lattice pattern is produced on the cheese's outer surface. The drying effect of refrigerated air during the maturation process causes the formation of a supple brownish rind which then acts to protect the cheese. At around six weeks of age the cheese is secured in plastic film which bears the Pastorello label.

Wines: Dry white wines; rosés.
Serve: End of meals with olives, red or green peppers and spring onions.
Fat content: 46 per cent.
Type: Bland/buttery.
Aroma: Unpronounced.

PECORINO ROMANO

Country of origin: Italy.

Background: Pecorino is the name given to all Italian cheeses made from sheep's milk. The best known and oldest is Pecorino Romano, so-called because it was first made near Rome. Pecorino Siciliano (also known as Canestrato) from Sicily and Pecorino Sardo from Sardinia are similar. When Pecorino Romano is made from cow's milk it is called Vacchino Romano; from goat's milk, Caprino Romano.

Description: Pecorino Romano is a hard Italian Grana cheese made in cylindrical shapes up to 25 cm (10 in) in diameter and some 23 cm (9 in) thick. Cheeses of this type can be aged for up to one year, when they become hard-textured, brittle and develop a smooth yellowish-whitish rind. The interiors are usually white to light yellow. The cheese's sheep milk origins show in its aroma; in taste it is sharply piquant, pronounced, distinctively 'sheepy'. It is used as a grating cheese, sometimes with, and sometimes as a substitute for, Parmesan.

Young Pecorino Romanos are softer, usually pure white, rather moist and crumbly. They are milder tasting than the aged versions but are still full and assertive, tangy—excellent uncomplicated rustic table cheeses.

Pepato is a Pecorino variety spiced with peppercorns enhancing further the sharp flavour of the cheese and complementing its hard granular texture.

Wines: Full-bodied reds.
Serve: Try the young Pecorino Romanos with garlic sausage, olives and crusty bread for a light meal. Aged cheeses are used for grating in many pasta-style dishes or in soufflés, omelettes and minestrone soups.
Fat content: Approximately 38 per cent.
Type: Sheep's milk/extra-hard grating cheese.
Aroma: Noticeable aroma of sheep's milk.

PECORINO SARDO

A sheep's milk cheese from Sardinia related to Pecorino Romano.
(See *Pecorino Romano*.)

PECORINO SICILIANO

A sheep's milk cheese from Sicily, primarily used for grating. Also known as Canestrato and related to Pecorino Romano.
(See *Pecorino Romano*.)

PEPATO

A variety of the Italian sheep's milk cheese Pecorino Romano. Pepato is spiced with peppercorns which further enhances the sharp

flavour of the cheese and complements its hard granular texture. The cheese is primarily used for grating.
(See *Pecorino Romano*.)

PEPERONI

This is the Danish cheese Blue Castello, minus the blue veining but studded with peppercorns. It has a 70 per cent fat content and is very rich and creamy with a spicy, peppery tang. Sold in 90 g (3 oz) small wheel shapes wrapped in plastic. Another variety is flavoured with chives.

PETIT SUISSE

Country of origin: France.

Background: This cheese was first made in the middle of last century. It gets its name from the Swiss employee of a country cheesemaker who suggested that cream should be added to a fresh, unripened cheese—hence Petit Suisse or 'Little Swiss' ('little' because of the size of the cheese, not the Swiss).

Description: This tiny cheese is made in the shape of a cylinder only 5 cm (2 in) long and 2.5 cm (1 in) in diameter. A fresh, unripened cheese with a high fat content, it is pure white in colour, rindless and extremely soft and creamy. It is usually marketed in a plastic container or wrapped in paper.
It is mild in flavour, with a faintly sourish tinge offsetting a delectable fresh creaminess. Freshness is the main point to watch for when buying this cheese; it must always be eaten fresh to appreciate its creamy delicacy. Petit Suisse will not last long and should be eaten as soon as possible after purchase.

Wines: Dry white wines, but goes equally well with tea or coffee.
Serve: An excellent dessert sprinkled with sugar and served with strawberries or similar fruit.
Fat content: 60-75 per cent.
Type: Fresh, unripened, double/triple crème.
Aroma: Unpronounced.

PHILADELPHIA

The name of America's best known cream cheese sold throughout the world. Despite its name it was originally produced in New York State in the late nineteenth century.
(See *Cream Cheese*.)

PICKLED CHEESE

Cheeses that are matured in a solution of salt and water or brine are often referred to as 'pickled' cheeses. The most notable example is Feta from Greece, but others include the Egyptian cheese Domiati and Brinza from the Balkans.

PINEAPPLE

This is an American Cheddar cheese which dates back to the middle of last century to Litchfield County, Connecticut. The cheese is so called because of its shape and because of the marks left on its rind from the loose mesh net in which it is matured. These marks resemble the scales of a pineapple.
(See *Cheddar*.)

PIPO CREM'

A soft, rich, mild and creamy popular French blue vein cheese. The cheese is produced in long cylindrical shapes about 10 cm (4 in) in diameter. The cheese is sold by the slice. A highly considered cheese, Pipo Crem' is related to Bleu de Bresse.
(See *Blue Veins*.)

POIVRE D'ANE

A variety of the French goat's milk cheese Banon, flavoured with herbs. The cheese is also known as Banon au Pebre d'Ai.
(See *Banon*.)

PONT L'EVEQUE

Country of origin: France.

Background: This is another cheese developed by French monks and is thought to be one of the oldest of the Normandy cheeses. It was written of in the thirteenth century when it was known as Angelot. Pont l'Evêque is matured in humid cellars whose walls or ceilings contain a special fungus which affects the cheese during its six-week maturing period. As this fungus is unique to the Pays d'Auge region where the cheese is made, Pont l'Evêque cannot be duplicated anywhere else.

Description: Pont l'Evêque is a small, square, washed-rind cheese about 10 cm (4 in) square and 2.5 cm (1 in) high, which comes boxed. The cheese weighs in the region of 375 g (12 oz). A smaller cheese 6 cm (2½ in) square by 2.5 cm (1 in) high is also made. It has a smooth, golden-yellow rind marked by crisscross patterns from the straw on which the cheese lies while it is maturing. The interior paste, which contains a few tiny holes, has a soft, almost honey-like texture, and is pale yellow in colour.

Pont l'Evêque has a unique taste, not pronounced or penetrating enough to be called strong, but rich, tangy and with a lingering distinctive aftertaste. It is an important cheese, rating number four in the French hierarchy (the first three are Roquefort, Brie and Camembert) but it is difficult to get in the peak of condition outside of France. Too often exported cheeses are past their prime and dry out, harden and develop a mouldy bitter taste. A good Pont l'Evêque should feel plump, resilient and supple; when cut the cheese should cling to the knife.

Vieux Pané is a large sized Pont l'Evêque. It comes in a 35 cm (14 in) square, 2.5 cm (1 in) thick. Its advantage is that because it is larger it does not dry out as quickly as the smaller Pont l'Evêque.

Wines: Full-bodied rich reds; in Normandy they sometimes eat it with cider; port or vintage sherry are also possibilities.
Serve: End of meals.
Fat content: 50 per cent.
Type: Monastery.

Aroma: Not overpronounced but noticeable and distinctive.

POONA

An American cheese first produced in New York State in the late 1940s. The cheese is made in a flat disc shape about 10 cm (4 in) in diameter and 5 cm (2 in) thick. It is soft, surface ripened and has a reddish surface smear —said to be rather like a mild Limburger in aroma.

POPCORN CHEESE

(See *Cottage Cheese.*)

PORT SALUT

Country of origin: France.

Background: One of the best-known of French cheeses, Port Salut (also known as Port du Salut) was created by Trappist monks who were domiciled in Switzerland after leaving France during the French Revolution. They returned to the Abbey of Nôtre Dame de Port du Salut (the name means 'place of safety') in the parish of Entrammes. By 1850 the monks were selling the cheese to visitors; its fame spread and when it went on the Paris market in 1873 it became an instant success.

Description: Port Salut is a semi-soft, pressed, washed-rind cheese made in discs measuring 20 cm to 23 cm (8-9 in) in diameter and some 5 cm (2 in) high. Made from cow's milk and matured for up to two months, the cheese has a thin orange rind and a creamy yellow interior, semi-soft, and resilient.

In taste Port Salut is initially mild, buttery, creamy and smooth flavoured with an attractive, lightly piquant aftertaste. Aged versions are, of course, more full-bodied with a deeper, fuller flavour.

The cheese has been widely copied both inside and outside France. In France the name is

Pont l'Evêque (photo by Russell Cockayne)

restricted to the use of one firm (S.A.F.R.) but numerous other firms produce Saint Paulin, a cheese very similar.

Wines: Fruity red wines.
Serve: A thoroughly satisfying snack-type cheese but also one that is likely to be enjoyed by most tastes if served at the end of a meal.
Fat content: 45-50 per cent.
Type: Monastery.
Aroma: Unpronounced.

POT CHEESE

Another name for Cottage Cheese.
(See *Cottage Cheese*.)

POULIGNY-SAINT-PIERRE

A French chèvre or goat's milk cheese made in the shape of a small pyramid.
(See *Chèvres*.)

PROCESSED CHEESE

By and large processed cheese has had a hard time at the hands of cheese writers. Variously described as the 'mongrels'[1] of the cheese world, a 'moron-like rindless child by sterilization out of tinfoil'[2] and 'solidified floor wax'[3], processed cheese has never been, and is not likely to be, placed in the gold medal class in international gourmet competitions.

Nevertheless, the humble processed cheese is enormously popular. In the USA, for example, it is estimated that one-third of the cheese made is processed. The reasons are obvious; the cheese is cheaper, it keeps well, it is easy to spread and slice, it will travel, melts easily, is nutritious and is bland to the point of innocuousness in flavour, unlikely to offend the most delicate of taste buds. This last point makes the cheese acceptable to children. Processed cheese is a good, economical, all-purpose family cheese.

[1]English food writer T. E. Layton.
[2]English wine and food expert Andre Simon.
[3]American cheese enthusiast Clifton Fadiman.

The reason that cheese buffs shudder gently at its name is that processed cheese has had its ripening process arrested at a given point by heat treatment. This means that the cheese can never develop the personality, character, individuality and flavour of natural cheese because the micro-organisms that help create these things have been effectively killed off.

Processed cheese is made by finely grinding, and mixing together by heating and stirring, one or more cheeses of the same or two or more varieties. An emulsifying agent is added and the result is a homogeneous plastic mass. Certain cheeses—Neufchâtel, Cottage, Creamed Cottage, cooked, hard grating, semi-soft, part skim, part skim spiced and skim milk cheeses —are not used. Lactic, citric, acetic or phosphoric acid or small amounts of cream, water, salt, colouring and spices or other flavouring materials may be added. The cheese may be smoked or it may be made from smoked cheese, or so-called liquid smoke flavour may be used. That description is taken practically verbatim from a US Department of Agriculture publication.

The history of processed cheese goes back to the early part of this century, being pioneered by the Swiss and eventually copied by cheese-producing countries throughout the world. Today vast amounts of processed Cheddar are manufactured, and there are also processed versions of Limburger, Gruyère, Emmentaler and the American Brick.

A marked trend has been the production of flavoured processed cheeses and cheese spreads. The following is just a sampling of some of the popular brand names and varieties sold on the world market.

AUVERNOIS (France): A processed Gruyère with either walnuts or almonds throughout as well as on the surface.

BAVARIAN (Germany): Flavoured with mushroom, pineapple, capsicum, chives, caraway, walnut, spring onion, garlic.

BAYERNLAND (Germany): Varieties flavoured with chives, mushroom, walnut, spices.

CREME CHERRY (Norway): Kirsch flavoured; another variety flavoured with walnut pieces.

A selection of mild-flavoured cheeses, predominantly processed cheeses

DANISH CHEF (Denmark): Varieties flavoured with fish, shrimp, crab, lobster, salmon, pepper, horseradish.

GOURMANDISE (France): Varieties flavoured with garlic, herb, port wine, cherry, walnut.

GRUNLAND (Germany): The trade name for a great range of processed cheeses—typical of the variety is the one studded with salami pieces particularly popular in the USA.

LAUGHING COW (France): Processed Gruyère in a large range of shapes and sizes.

RAMBOL (France): Walnut flavoured or with pieces of walnut impressed in it; there is also a peppered version.

REGAL PICON (France): Flavoured with cherry, kirsch, walnut pieces, green pepper.

SAMOS 90 (France): Spreads flavoured with mushroom, raisins, walnuts.

TIGER (Switzerland): Flavours of celery, caraway, mustard.

And so on. It is fair to say there is a flavoured processed cheese or spread available to suit almost any taste. It is also fair to say that the taste sensation you get when eating such a cheese is that of the flavouring additive. The cheese itself sits quietly in the background—mild, innocuous, rather plastic and undemanding.

PROVOLETTI

A member of the pasta filata family of Italian cheeses. Aged varieties of these cheeses are used in cooking. This cheese is essentially a small sized Provolone.
(See *Pasta Filata* and *Provolone*.)

PROVOLONE

Country of origin: Italy.

Background: Provolone, made from cow's milk, is a latter-day descendant of the Italian cheese Caciocavallo. Both are pasta filata or drawn curd cheeses. Provolone originated in southern Italy but is now made in several other countries, including America and Australia.

Description: This cheese can take a variety of shapes such as a truncated cone, a pear, a sausage or a cylinder. On its surface it often bears the marks or indentations left by the cords from which it hangs, in pairs, while maturing. Provolone, which is smoked, has a firm, smooth, shiny, golden yellow rind and a cream white interior free of holes. It is a supple-textured cheese which cuts cleanly and evenly without any flaking or crumbling. Young Provolones (those matured for between two and three months) are milder tasting than the aged variety, but still distinctive, and are used as table cheeses. The older versions (aged up to six months and longer) are often used as grating and cooking cheese. These cheeses are more granular in texture, more robust in flavour and saltier.
    As Provolone undergoes a 'cheddaring' process when it is made it is also related to the Cheddar family.
    Provolones are normally made in weights from 3.5 kg to 6 kg (8-14 lb). The pear shaped variety is the most common. Larger sized cheeses which can weigh up to 90 kg (200 lb) are known as Provolone Giganti.

Wines: Reds such as chianti.
Serve: As a table cheese Provolone goes well with bread and biscuits, pineapple wedges, dried apricots, red and green peppers and spring onions. Grated it can be used as a grilled topping to hamburgers, chicken pieces or veal or as a stuffing for ravioli, canneloni or as a melted topping to pizzas. Coated with egg and breadcrumbs and quickly pan-fried till crisp and golden brown, Provolone makes a delicious snack or appetiser.
Fat content: 45 per cent.
Type: Grating cheese/Cheddar.
Aroma: Unpronounced.

PYRAMIDE

Several French goat's milk cheeses or *chèvres* are called Pyramide because they are made in the shape of a small pyramid with the top cut off. Valençay, Levroux and Pouligny Saint Pierre are three such cheeses; some types are coated with wood ashes.

Another variety marketed as Pyramide White and Black has a thin, edible crust with a soft, ivory white interior paste. Such cheeses are generally at the mild flavoured end of the French *chèvres* range.
(See *Valencay*.)

QUARDO

Another name for the stracchino style Italian cheese, Milano.
(See *Stracchino* and *Milano*.)

QUARK

A type of fresh, unripened Cottage Cheese made in Europe. Such Continental-style Cottage Cheeses appear as a solid mass rather than as a mass of separate curd particles. Widely used in cooking.
(See *Cottage Cheese*.)

QUART

A type of Maroilles—a strong smelling, gamy and pungent tasting French washed rind cheese.
(See *Maroilles*.)

QUESO ANEJO

This is a Mexican skim-milk cheese which is matured for periods up to eight months. (The name means 'aged cheese'.) The cheese itself is dry, white and has a rather crumbly texture.

In Mexico it is sometimes served with enchiladas. When covered with red chili powder it is known as Queso Enchilado.

QUESO BLANCO

This cheese is made throughout South America under a variety of names and in a variety of styles. Types are made from whole cow's milk and skimmed milk; some versions are smoked. In its many varieties the cheese can appear as a cottage cheese, cream cheese, grating cheese or a firm textured table cheese. Essentially it's the same cheese but the different manufacturing methods, maturing times, sizes and shapes result in a range of flavours and textures. The name means 'white cheese'.

RACLETTE

Country of origin: Switzerland.

Background: A cheese from the Canton of Valais and therefore often known as Valais Raclette. This cheese is used in a special toasted dish called raclette. The dish and the cheese take their name from the French *racler*—'to scrape'.

Description: Raclette is made in wheel shapes up to 9 kg (20 lb). The cheese has a light-brown natural rind with a firm textured interior, pale yellow to light brown in colour, which is scattered with holes. Like all the major Swiss cheeses Raclette is a hard, pressed cooked cheese. It is made from cow's milk and matured for up to six months.

As a table cheese Raclette is mild but distinctive, rather nut-like, palatable and tasty. It can be compared to Gruyère.

Wines: Dry white wines; can also go with beer.
Serve: As a table cheese at end of meals. When used in raclette, the cheese is placed on a heated griddle until it begins to melt, then, when sizzling, it is scooped off with a knife onto toast placed alongside the griddle. Traditionally the cheese was scraped onto boiled potatoes.

Fat content: 50 per cent.
Type: Swiss.
Aroma: Unpronounced.

RAGNIT

A cheese first produced by Dutch settlers in the region of Tilsit in east Prussia last century. It is more commonly known as Tilsit.
(See *Tilsit*.)

RAMBOL

A French processed cheese range flavoured with, and often studded with, nuts.
(See *Processed Cheese*.)

REBLOCHON

Country of origin: France.

Background: This is a centuries-old cheese from the Savoy mountain area of France. Herdsmen tending the cows would leave enough milk for a second milking on the days when the milk quotas were checked. The herdsmen would milk the cows for a second time after the inspection, keeping the results of this milking (what they considered to be the 'richest' milk) for themselves. It was from this practice that Reblochon developed and took its name. *Reblocher* means 'second milking'.

Description: Reblochon is a soft, surface-ripened, washed-rind cheese made in flat discs about 12.5 cm (5 in) in diameter and 2.5 cm (1 in) thick. It has a reddish-coloured outer rind, smooth with a matt finish, and a pale creamy interior. The cheese is matured for about four weeks.

A very attractive cheese, essentially mild tasting but creamy, yielding, vaguely nutty—held in high esteem by cheese buffs. At its best it should feel supple and plump. Past its prime it develops a bitter taste.

Wines: Light and fruity beaujolais style reds.
Serve: End of meals.
Fat content: 50 per cent.
Type: Monastery.
Aroma: Unpronounced.

RECUIT

A whey, Cottage style cheese, the best known version of which is Ricotta.
(See *Ricotta*.)

RED CHESHIRE

A Cheshire cheese treated with an annatto dye which gives it its reddish colouring—originally carrot juice was used. Cheshire comes in three varieties, red, white and blue—a very patriotic cheese.
(See *Cheshire*.)

REDSKIN

(See American *Cheddars*.)

REGAL PICON

A well-known brand name for a range of French processed cheese which can be flavoured with kirsch, walnut pieces or green peppers.
(See *Processed Cheese*.)

REMOUDOU

A Belgian cheese related to Limburger and Hervé. All three are washed rind cheeses and are noted for their pungent aromas. Both Remoudou and Hervé have a highly pronounced gamy taste.
(See *Hervé*.)

Red Cheshire (photo by Russell Cockayne)

REYBIER

Brand name for a large range of French processed cheese. Flavourings vary, but include herbs, kirsch, pepper, hazelnuts, almonds and a smoked variety.
(See *Processed Cheese*.)

RICOTTA

Country of origin: Italy.

Background: This cheese, sometimes known as 'whey' or 'albumin' cheese, is a type of Italian Cottage Cheese.

Description: Ricotta is made from the whey drained from the cheese curd when making Provolone. Although liquid, the whey still contains a protein known as lactalbumin. When heated the whey coagulates in a similar fashion to the white of an egg. Acids such as vinegar are added and often extra milk also to improve the balance, fat content and quality of the cheese. The cheese is made from cow's milk and does not undergo a ripening process. Pure white in colour, Ricotta has a fine, slightly moist texture and a bland, sweetish flavour. It comes as a smooth white mass and is packaged in a variety of shapes, sizes, tubs and containers. As with all fresh, unripened cheeses, Ricotta does not have a long life and should be used within a short time of purchase. The cheese can be cured and salted, when it becomes Dry Ricotta, used as a grating cheese.

Ricotta-style cheese is made in various parts of Europe under a variety of names such as Ziger, Sérac, Brocotte, Mejette, Schottenziger and Recuit.

American Ricotta, made chiefly in Wisconsin and New York, has between 5 and 10 per cent whole or skimmed milk added to it. The whole milk is used in fresh Ricotta which tends to be creamier and sweeter than the Italian version; skimmed milk for Dry Ricotta.

Ricotta Salata is a hard, flaky version made in a ball-shape and used in salads in a similar way to Feta.

Australian Ricotta is made in several states. The cheese is often marketed in parchment wrapped portions or in plastic containers of 500 g (1 lb).

Wines: Light whites, reds, rosés or coffee, depending on how the cheese is used.
Serve: Ricotta is well suited as a base for a variety of sweet and savoury dishes. It can be used as a dessert cheese, sprinkled with sugar and eaten with fresh fruit; as a health food lunch or a snack with dried fruits and chopped nuts intermixed and muesli added to thicken it. To make an interesting cheese dip try it with a packet of onion soup made to half strength, or with an equal portion of blue vein cheese and some fresh herbs, or with curry powder and yoghurt.
Fat content: 4-10 per cent.
Type: Whey cheese, fresh, unripened.
Aroma: Unpronounced.

RICOTTA SALATA

A hard Ricotta, very flaky, made in ball shapes weighing just over 2 kg (up to 5 lb). The cheese is used in salads in a similar fashion to Feta.
(See *Ricotta*.)

RIDDER

Country of origin: Norway.

Background: This cheese is a Norwegian version of Saint Paulin.

Description: Ridder is usually marketed in small wheel shapes some 23 cm (9 in) in diameter. The cheese has a wax rind and is pale yellow in colour. The interior paste is firm and supple-textured, dotted with small holes.

Made from cow's milk, its flavour is mild, smooth and creamy with a lightly piquant aftertaste. In texture, taste and bouquet it can be considered a creamier version (the cheese has a higher fat content) of Saint Paulin.

Wines: Burgundy-style reds.
Serve: End of meals or as a snack.
Fat content: 60 per cent.
Type: Monastery/double crème.
Aroma: Unpronounced.

RIVIANA

One of two Camembert style cheeses made in Australia. Riviana comes from New South Wales. The other Australian Camembert is Moe from Victoria.
(See *Camembert*.)

ROBIOLA

An Italian stracchino style cheese which is made in two sizes, the smaller one being the stronger tasting.
(See *Stracchino*.)

ROLLOT

A soft, washed rind cheese made in small flat cylinder shapes measuring 7.5 cm (3 in) in diameter and 2.5 cm (1 in) thick. This is quite a spicy, full flavoured French cheese with a noticeable aroma similar in some ways to Pont l'Evêque. Rollot is a cheese not usually encountered outside France.
(See *Pont l'Evêque*.)

ROMADUR

Country of origin: Germany.

Background: This cheese, which is chiefly produced in Bavaria, falls in what the Germans call the *roschmier* range—soft cheeses with a reddish tinge. These are surface-ripened, washed-rind cheeses whose surface is smeared with a mould-producing bacteria. Limburger is the best-known cheese of this type.

Description: The cheese is marketed in sizes weighing from 125 g ($\frac{1}{4}$ lb) up to 500 g (1 lb). It is made in bar and square shapes, a standard size being 12.5 cm (5 in) long and 5 cm (2 in) square. Romadur is made from whole or partly skimmed cow's milk and has a smooth rind with a yellowish-brown to reddish tinge. The interior is pale yellow with a few holes.

Romadur can be compared to Limburger but it contains less salt, is ripened for a shorter period (up to five weeks) at a lower temperature and has a smaller degree of surface bacterial smear. Consequently neither the flavour nor the aroma is as pronounced as that of Limburger. All in all, a milder Limburger style cheese.

Wines: Full-bodied reds, beer.
Serve: A good snack type cheese.
Fat content: Approximately 47 per cent.
Type: Monastery.
Aroma: Noticeable, but not over-pronounced.

ROMANO

A hard Italian grating cheese which is also known as Incanestrato. When made from sheep's milk it is known as Pecorino Romano; from cow's milk Vacchino Romano and from goat's milk Caprino Romano. Sardo Romano is a version made in Sardinia. When these cheeses are cured for less than a year they are used as table cheeses.
(See *Pecorino Romano*.)

RONDELE

A range of double crème cheeses which are flavoured with pepper, garlic and herbs; an unflavoured version is also available. All are rich and creamy, with the flavouring agents providing a tang.
(See *Double Crèmes*.)

ROQUEFORT

Country of origin: France.

Background: Of all the blue-veined cheeses, this is the oldest and to many minds the best. Throughout recorded history it has certainly not lacked for notable propagandists. Pliny the Elder thought it the best cheese in Rome two thousand years ago and it was a great favourite of the Emperor Charlemagne in the eighth century. Even Casanova got in on the act, extolling its excellence and writing that it 'revived love' and 'brought to maturity a budding love'.

The cheese comes from the Causes, an area of limestone plateaux in the province of Aquitaine. It is made from unskimmed sheep's milk and matured in limestone caves.

The story goes that in times past a shepherd accidentally left a piece of sheep's milk cheese with some bread in one of the caves. When he came upon the cheese and bread some weeks later they had formed into one monstrous, coagulated, mould-covered mass—but it didn't taste bad!

Description: Roquefort has its curd treated with *Penicillium roqueforti*, which is found in rye bread, to develop its veining. The unique atmospheric conditions of the limestone caves in which the cheese ripens for between three and five months do the rest.

Roquefort is a cylindrical cheese with a thin, almost transparent crust. It is creamy white in colour and is marbled by a network of blue veining running through its body. The cheese measures approximately 17.5 cm (7 in) in diameter and 10 cm (4 in) in height.

Roquefort is a strong-tasting blue vein, very rich, pungent and salty, leaving a sharp sensation on the tongue and a lingering aftertaste. Exported cheeses are often too sharp and salty for some tastes, but many connoisseurs hold it to be the finest cheese in the world.

The cheese takes its name from Roquefort-sur-Soulzon where it is made.

Wines: Strong, rich red wines; port.
Serve: End of meals; if too salty mix a little butter into the cheese.
Fat content: 45 per cent.
Type: Blue vein/sheep's milk.
Aroma: Mould smell, noticeable but not over-pronounced.

ROSCHMIER

This is not an individual cheese but the word used to describe a range of German cheeses—soft cheeses with a reddish tinge. They are all washed rind cheeses, many of them quite sharp tasting.
(See *Romadur*.)

ROYALP

Country of origin: Switzerland.

Background: This is a relatively new cheese, made in eastern Switzerland and now being promoted as one of the 'big five' Swiss cheeses (the others are Emmentaler, Gruyère, Appenzell and Sbrinz).

Description: Royalp is made in wheel shapes measuring 25 cm (10 in) in diameter and 8 cm (3 in) deep. The cheese has a reddish-brown semi-hard natural rind and a softer interior paste peppered with small holes. Made from cow's milk, it is ripened for three months. In flavour it is mild but distinctive, with a piquancy in its aftertaste. By the time Royalp has reached its export markets it has normally become stronger tasting, rather like a more full-flavoured Gruyère.

Wines: Fruity reds, rosés, also beer.
Serve: A good table cheese which goes well with a variety of fruits and nuts, or in sandwiches; the cheese has good melting qualities and makes an excellent Welsh rarebit.
Fat content: 45 per cent.
Type: Swiss.
Aroma: Unpronounced.

SAANEN

This is a Swiss grating cheese similar to Sbrinz. Such cheeses can be matured for up to seven years. They taste like a very full, very matured Gruyère.
(See *Sbrinz*.)

SAGA

A rich, creamy double crème cheese from Denmark with a moulded surface and internal blue veining. The blue vein flavour is mild; the cheese is similar to Blue Castello in style and has a 70 per cent fat content.
(See *Blue Castello* and *Bavarian Blue*.)

Sbrinz (top), Royalp (below)

SAGE

Certain Cheddars which are spiced with sage are known by this name. Two of the best known are Vermont Sage (American) and Derby Sage (English). The cheeses have a greenish hue.
(See *Cheddar*.)

SAINT ANDRE

A French triple crème with a 75 per cent fat content. The cheese has a light bloomy white 'fluffy' rind, a rich, creamy, tangy flavour and texture and a noticeable bouquet.
(See *Triple Crèmes*.)

SAINT BENOIT

A small disc shaped French cheese about 7.5 cm (3 in) in diameter with a bloomy rind and soft, creamy paste. St Benoit belongs to the Brie/Camembert family and is made in two versions: with a 40 per cent and 60 per cent fat content. It is similar to Coulommiers.
(See *Coulommiers*.)

SAINT MARCELLIN

Country of origin: France.

Background: This cheese dates back to the fifteenth century. It was supposed to have been offered to the future King Louis XI after he had been rescued from a bear by two charcoal-burners in the Lenta Forest. Louis liked it so much that it was later served at the royal table.

Description: Saint Marcellin is a small, disc-shaped cheese no more than 7.5 cm (3 in) in diameter and 2.5 cm (1 in) thick. It is a soft cheese with a light natural rind or crust on which a blue-greyish mould has been cultivated. The cheese's soft interior paste is not affected by the mould so it is not classed as a blue vein. Saint Marcellin is mild tasting but tangy with a pleasantly creamy, vaguely 'goaty' flavour. It is ripened for about one month before marketing when it often appears wrapped in chestnut leaves. The cheese was originally produced on farms and made from goat's milk but is now commercially manufactured from cow's milk.

Wines: Light and fruity reds.
Serve: End of meals.
Fat content: 50 per cent.
Type: Bland/buttery.
Aroma: Unpronounced.

SAINT MAURE

Country of origin: France.

Description: This is a French goat's milk cheese made in small cylinder shapes about 15 cm (6 in) long and 2.5 cm (1 in) in diameter. Those produced on farms have a bluish rind while the commercially made varieties have a white bloomy rind. Such cheeses are ripened for one month and have a soft creamy texture and a full, fresh 'goaty' flavour to them. Older cheeses develop a very ripe odour and flavour.

Wines: Fruity reds and whites.
Serve: End of meals.
Fat content: 45 per cent.
Type: Goat's milk.
Aroma: Lightly 'goaty'; aged cheeses are quite pungent.

SAINT NECTAIRE

Country of origin: France.

Background: This is a highly rated cheese which is made in the Auvergne province of France and is believed to date back to the Middle Ages.

Description: Saint Nectaire is made from cow's milk in flat disc shapes measuring 20 cm (8 in) in diameter and 3 cm (1½ in) thick. The

cheese has a natural rind, greyish-white and often scattered with yellow and red moulds. Saint Nectaire is a semi-soft cheese with a firm but supple interior paste light yellow in colour. The cheese is matured for two months.

Saint Nectaire is not a strong tasting cheese but it has a pleasant tang and a lingering aftertaste, rather subtle and quite distinctive.

Wines: Light fruity reds and whites.
Serve: A distinctive cheese to serve at end of meals.
Fat content: 45 per cent.
Type: Monastery,
Aroma: Noticeable mould smell.

SAINT OTHO

Country of origin: Switzerland.

Description: This is a low fat content cheese which is made from skimmed milk and matured for up to four months. A hard, pressed cheese with a natural orange hued rind, it has a firm, supple texture and an interior paste which varies from ivory to yellow in colour. Small different sized holes dot its interior. The cheese is made in a wheel shape weighing about 7 kg (15 lb).

Saint Otho has the nutty background typical of Swiss-style cheeses but is somewhat waxy in comparison to other types, lacking the depth and complexity of its more famous relatives—quite bland and mild. A good cheese, though, for those concerned with their intake of fats as its fat content ranks amongst the lowest of all natural cheeses.

Wines: Light reds and whites.
Serve: General, all purpose eating cheese.
Fat content: 9 per cent.
Type: Swiss.
Aroma: Unpronounced.

SAINT PAULIN

The forebear of Saint Paulin is Port Salut. In France, Port Salut is a restricted trade name but several companies produce Saint Paulin.

As a name and style of cheese, it appears to be becoming more popular and better known than Port Salut throughout the world. The cheese is made in small wheel shapes. It has a semi-soft texture, a thin orange coloured washed rind and its flavour varies with the brand purchased and its age. Saint Paulin can be mild, bland and buttery or tangy and fulsome with a lingering and richly distinctive aftertaste.
(See *Port Salut.*)

SAMOS 90

Brand name for a French range of processed cheese.
(See *Processed Cheese.*)

SAMSOE

Country of origin: Denmark.

Background: This is Denmark's most popular cheese, named after the island of Samsoe. Samsoe stands at the head of a family of Danish cheeses, all related in taste and texture but varying in shape and size. In Denmark this cheese is the national favourite, as popular as Cheddar in England.

Description: Samsoe is a rich golden coloured cheese made in the shape of a large disc 44 cm (18 in) in diameter and approximately 10 cm (4 in) in height, or square, 38 cm by 38 cm (15 x 15 in). It has a dry yellow rind (sometimes wax-coated), a firm, supple texture and is pure yellow to white in colour, containing a limited number of regularly shaped holes from pea to cherry size.

Samsoe is a bland and buttery type of cheese with a mild, sweetish, nutlike flavour. It is matured for about five months but when aged longer the cheese develops a more full-bodied pungency. The cheese is made from cow's milk.

Wines: Light reds and whites.
Serve: A good all-purpose table cheese, liked

Samsoe, and King Christian IX, a spiced cheese

by children because of its mildness. It can be coarsely grated or thinly sliced for cooking.
Fat content: 45 per cent.
Type: Bland/buttery.
Aroma: Unpronounced.

SAPSAGO

Country of origin: Switzerland.

Background: This is a hard grating cheese whose antecedents are believed to date back to the fifteenth century. One theory has it that the cheese was first developed by Irish monks, domiciled in Switzerland, who made the cheese with four-leaf clover.

Description: Sapsago is an unusual cheese, light-green in colour, which is made from soured skimmed cow's milk combined with whole milk. During the making process, quantities of dried clover are added to the curd which give the cheese its colour and its unique taste, quite sharp and pronounced, the clover adding an aromatic herb-like quality.

Sapsago is made in cone-shapes no more than 7.5 cm (3 in) in diameter at its base, and 10 cm (4 in) tall. The cheese has no rind and a hard, dry texture. It is matured for between three to five months.

Sapsago is also made in Germany and is known by several other names such as Green Cheese, Schabziger, Krauterkäse and Glarner-käse.

Wines: Full-bodied red or white wines.
Serve: Normally used as a grating cheese.
Fat content: 5-9 per cent.
Type: Spiced, extra-hard grating cheese.
Aroma: Noticeable aroma of clover.

SARDO

Also known as Pecorino Sardo, this is a sheep's milk cheese which is the Sardinian version of Pecorino Romano.
(See *Pecorino Romano*.)

SBRINZ

Country of origin: Switzerland.

Background: This is primarily a grating cheese, the oldest of the Swiss cheeses, believed to have been known in Roman times.

Description: Sbrinz is made in the shape of a large flattened wheel in weights which vary from about 18 kg (40 lb) to 40 kg (90 lb). The cheese usually measures about 55 cm (22 in) in diameter. The rind is dry, smooth, hard and yellow to brown in colour. Its interior is dark yellow with a dense, close texture which may contain one or two small holes. Sbrinz, made from cow's milk, is matured for eighteen months to three years, which makes it a hard, brittle cheese ideally suited for grating. The cheese has little aroma but a rich, mellow flavour, sharp and tangy.

Young, softer cheeses, not suitable for grating, are known as Spalen from the wooden containers which are used to transport them.

Saanen, also Swiss, is a similar grating cheese to Sbrinz. It can be aged for as long as seven years and tastes like a very full, well matured Gruyère.

Wines: Light whites and fruity reds.
Serve: An excellent grating cheese which can be used for seasoning soups and sauces, rice, polenta and pasta; when used as a table cheese Sbrinz is broken off in pieces or shaved off in thin slivers, rather than cut.
Fat content: 45-50 per cent.
Type: Swiss/extra-hard grating cheese.
Aroma: Unpronounced.

SCARMORZA

Country of origin: Italy.

Background: This is an old Italian cheese related to Mozzarella and Provolone. It was formerly made from buffalo's milk, but today is chiefly made from cow's milk. Like Mozzarella and Provolone, it is a drawn curd cheese (*pasta filata*).

Description: Scarmorza is a small, soft, oval-shaped cheese about the size of a lemon, yellowish in colour with a firm but supple texture.

The cheese can be eaten fresh when its taste is mild with a delicate sweetish, nutty flavour. Older cheeses, which are sharper tasting, are used for cooking.

Wines: Light fruity reds; dry whites such as white hermitage.
Serve: Young Scarmorzas can be used as table cheeses, as snacks, or at the end of a meal; the more matured versions (those aged for between 4-6 weeks) are used as cooking cheeses, particularly in pizzas.
Fat content: 45 per cent.
Type: Fresh, unripened.
Aroma: Unpronounced.
(See *Pasta Filata*.)

SCHABZIGER

A German version of the Swiss grating cheese Sapsago, notable for the fact that it is light green in colour.
(See *Sapsago*.)

SCHMIERKASE

(See *Cottage Cheese*.)

SCHNITTKASE

The name, which means 'sliceable' cheese, is given to a group of cheeses produced in Germany which are considered suitable for slicing. They are all based on cheeses developed in other countries, apart from Tilsit, which was first produced in East Prussia. In fact, Tilsit has Dutch antecedents, having been created by immigrants from the Netherlands.

The Schnittkäse group comprises German Edam, Geheimratskäse (a smaller sized Edam), Trappist (similar to Port Salut), Tilsit (a stronger Port Salut style) and German Gouda.

SCHOTTENZIGER

A whey, Cottage style cheese, the best known version of which is Ricotta.
(See *Ricotta*.)

SCHWEIZER

This Swiss cheese is made in the shape of a small loaf and is one of the stronger tasting Gruyère type cheeses. It has an immediate flavour that dominates the palate at first bite —strong and intense.
(See *Gruyère*.)

SELLES-SUR-CHER

A young French goat's milk cheese with a charcoal powdered natural rind. The cheese is ripened for a three week period and is soft textured and mild with a noticeably nutty flavour. It is made in small 150 g (5 oz) ball shapes.
(See *Chèvres*.)

SEPTMONCEL

A French blue vein also known as Gex or Bleu du Haut Jura.
(See *Bleu du Haut Jura*.)

SERAC

A whey, Cottage style cheese, the best known version of which is Ricotta.
(See *Ricotta*.)

SERRA DA ESTRELLA

Country of origin: Portugal.

Background: This cheese is considered the best of a range of Portuguese mountain cheeses. All Serra cheeses are mountain cheeses; many

carry in addition the name of the district or mountain range in which they are made—as with Serra da Estrella.

Description: The cheese is made in thick disc shapes up to 30 cm (10 in) in diameter and 5 cm (2 in) thick. It has a compact, semi-firm texture and its cream-white interior paste is dotted with a few small holes.

The cheese is made from sheep's milk but can be made from a mixture of sheep's and goat's milk; occasionally it is made from cow's milk. One of the interesting features of this cheese is that no animal rennet is used to coagulate the milk—this is effected by an extract from a certain type of thistle.

One of the best of the European sheep's milk cheeses, Serra da Estrella is comparable to the highly rated Spanish cheese Manchego. Ripened for only a two to three week period, the cheese is essentially mild tasting yet distinctively 'sheepy', faintly piquant, oily and attractive.

Wines: Dry reds.
Serve: Snacks; an arresting and distinctive cheese for a cheese board.
Fat content: 40 per cent.
Type: Sheep's milk.
Aroma: Unpronounced.

SLIPCOTE

An English version of Cream Cheese popular in Shakespeare's time.
(See *Cream Cheese*.)

SMOKED CHEESE

Smoked cheese is not a type, but simply a variety, often Cheddar or Emmentaler, which has been flavoured by smoke. In many cases the smoke flavouring is artificially created by chemicals rather than the cheese being naturally smoked over a fire. The traditional shape of smoked cheese is that of a long sausage.

Much of the smoked cheese on the market today is processed, with flavours ranging from mild to sharpish. They are often spiced with herbs such as caraway, and other additives.

SORBAIS

A version of Maroilles, a strong smelling and pungent tasting French washed rind cheese. (See *Maroilles*.)

SOUR CURD CHEESE

Country of origin: Germany.

Background: As the name implies, these are a range of German cheeses made from the curd of skimmed sour milk. Such cheeses have the virtue of a high protein content coupled with a low fat content. Their lack of virtue for many people is that they are often extremely pronounced in taste and smell. Although the numerous varieties range in flavour from mild to extremely sharp, they are all somewhat an acquired taste.

This type of cheese has been made in Germany for more than two hundred years and the Germans take to them with great gusto, eating them with and in beer, sometimes with cider, using them to complement such delicacies as goose-dripping on bread and sometimes covering them with a mixture of vinegar-oil dressing, onions and paprika.

Description: The two best-known sour curd cheeses are Harz and Mainz. They are small, disc shaped, rubbery-textured cheeses with smooth, golden yellow to reddish-brown surfaces and pale glassy yellow interiors.

Other types are Stängen (bar), Hand (hand), Bauerhand (peasant hand), Korb (basket), Spitz (pointed) and Olmützer Quargel. (Quargel is a general name for sour curd cheeses.) Most of these are round and flat, sometimes covered with an edible mould. Spitz is flavoured with caraway seeds. Olmützer Quargel, noted for its sharpness, comes from Bavaria.

Kochkäse (cooked cheese) is produced by heating pre-ripened curd. It is mostly sold in tins or plastic containers. The cheese is very pure tasting and spreads easily.

Wines: This type of cheese goes best with beer, sometimes cider.
Serve: As a snack.

A selection of Smoked Cheeses

Fat content: Less than 10 per cent.
Type: Strong smelling.
Aroma: Pronounced.
(See *Harz* and *Mainz.*)

SOUTHBROOK CHESHIRE

Origin: Australia.

Background: A Cheshire style cheese made since 1964, in the town of Southbrook, Queensland, a few kilometres south-west of Toowoomba. This is the only Cheshire type cheese now manufactured in Australia.

Description: A crumbly textured cheese with a slight acidic tang that develops to a pronounced bite as the cheese matures. Its pale cream colour results from the high acidity of the manufacturing process. Maturing takes up to three months before sealing in 250 g ($\frac{1}{2}$ lb), 500 g (1 lb) and 2.5 kg ($5\frac{1}{2}$ lb) plastic packs.

Wines: Rich burgundies, claret; the milder flavour of a lightly matured Southbrook Cheshire suits a rosé or riesling. For cooking, it can be used as a substitute for matured natural Cheddar.
Serve: End of meals with dried apricots, figs and grapes.
Fat content: 48 per cent.
Type: Cheddar.
Aroma: Unpronounced.

SPALEN

This is a younger version of the Swiss grating cheese Sbrinz. Spalens are so called because of the wooden containers that are used to transport them. Unlike Sbrinz, they are not used for grating, but as table cheeses.
(See *Sbrinz.*)

SPICED CHEESE

Spiced cheeses cover a large range of flavours and types. Notable ones include: Lancashire Sage, a Cheddar-style cheese flavoured with sage (its American equivalent is Vermont Sage); the Dutch cheese Leyden flavoured with cumin and caraway seeds; and Friesian spiced with cloves (as is the Norwegian cheese Nokkelost). The Swiss grating cheese Sapsago has had clover added to it while the English have taken to flavouring several of their traditional cheeses with wine, cider, beer and chives. Boursin is a spiced triple crème while there is a host of processed cheeses flavoured or spiced with additives ranging from salmon to pineapple.

SPICED GOUDA

A variety of the Dutch cheese Gouda spiced with cumin seed.
(See *Gouda.*)

SPITZ

This is a member of the range of German sour curd cheeses noted for their low fat content, high protein value, full aroma and penetrating flavour. Spitz is a variety spiced with caraway seed.
(See *Sour Curd Cheeses, Harz* and *Mainz.*)

STANGEN

One of the range of German sour curd cheeses. The name means 'bar cheese'. These cheeses are small, rubbery textured, with smooth, golden yellow to reddish brown surfaces and pale glassy yellow interiors. They can be extremely pronounced in both taste and aroma; even mild varieties are quite distinctive and all are something of an acquired taste.
(See *Sour Curd Cheeses, Harz* and *Mainz.*)

STEINBUSCHER

Country of origin: Germany.

Background: This is a cheese first produced in northern Germany last century. It takes its

name from the town where it was first developed.

Description: Steinbüscher is a cheese of the same style as Limburger, although not so full-flavoured or spicy in aroma. It is made in squares varying in weight from 200 g to 1 kg (7 oz-2¼ lb). The cheese has a reddish-brown outer rind covered with a layer of white mould, and a straw yellow interior with few holes.

The Germans place this cheese in their semi-soft, sliceable range of cheeses, which include Wilstermarsch, Edelpilz, Butter Cheese or Damenkäse and Weisslacker. Steinbüscher has a rich, buttery consistency and is at the bland end of the range—a mild-tasting German cheese only lightly piquant in taste.

Wines: Light dry whites, light reds.
Serve: End of meals, snacks.
Fat content: 50 per cent.
Type: Monastery/mild.
Aroma: Unpronounced.

STILTON

Country of origin: Great Britain (England).

Background: The 'king' of cheeses in the opinion of many experts, Stilton was first sold over two hundred years ago to coach passengers who stopped at the Bell Inn in Stilton Village in Huntingdonshire. Now recognised as one of the greatest cheeses in the world, Stilton has the distinction of being the only English cheese with a trade copyright. Stiltons are only made in parts of Leicestershire, Derbyshire and Nottinghamshire.

Description: Stilton is a blue-vein cheese, semi-firm, made from the best cream and milk. Creamy white in colour, it matures in three to six months. Immature Stiltons do not take on the network of blue veins which is created in the cheese by injection of a *Penicillium* spore. These immature cheeses are known as White Stiltons.

The cheese is made from cow's milk enriched with cream, in the shape of a tall cylinder some 15 cm (6 in) in diameter and 25 cm (10 in) high. It has a brown-greyish rind, slightly wrinkled from surface bacterial activity. The internal blue veining is dense and evenly distributed, a sign of quality in any blue vein cheese.

In flavour Stilton is distinctively piquant but rich and mellow with clean Cheddar undertones. It is not as salty as the French Roquefort and is less creamy than Gorgonzola.

To appreciate it at its best, you must look after it well. The Stilton Manufacturers' Association states that the cheese should be kept at room temperature, covered with a cloth. A cheese that has gone dry should be covered with a cloth dampened with brine (a handful of common salt in a basin of water). Stiltons can be kept in a refrigerator but for best results keep them wrapped in a damp cloth.

A widespread fallacy is that Stilton is improved by mixing port wine into it. This is a practice which dates back to Victorian times. It spoils the cheese while adding nothing to the rich succulence of the Stilton flavour. The Stilton Manufacturers' Association maintains that if the cheese is good it does not require port, and if it is a bad cheese, no amount of port is going to improve its flavour.

Wines: Port or any full-bodied burgundy.
Serve: End of meals.
Fat content: 55 per cent.
Type: Blue vein.
Aroma: Noticeable mould smell.

STRACCHINO

Stracchino is a generic name for a range of Italian cheeses, usually rich, soft, white cheese, virtually rindless, designed to be eaten fresh. Cheeses of this sort have been made since the twelfth century.

The name is derived from the word *stracca* (dialect for 'tired') and referred to the condition of cows making the long trek south over the Lombardy Plains before winter. The fact that the cows were fatigued affected the quality of their milk. Although the same situation does not exist today, the name stracchino lives on.

There are two types of stracchino—*piccante* (sharp) and *dolce* (mild). Most stracchino cheeses are ripened for short periods of ten to fifteen days and are so fresh and delicate that they rarely leave Italy.

Gorgonzola (a *piccante* type) and Taleggio are two exceptions, but both are ripened for a longer period. To add to the confusion, Stracchino is the name of a specific cheese as well as the generic name for a range.

Cheeses of this type include Crescenza (very rich, and so soft and creamy that it can be spread like butter) and Robiola (made in two sizes, the smaller being sharp-tasting). The actual cheese known as Stracchino is of the *dolce* variety—white, moist, with a plastic consistency to its texture, milky with a light tang.

SUPREME DES DUCS

A double crème produced in Neufchâtel-en-Bray. More commonly known as Suprême, the cheese is made in a small thick disc shape with a natural bloomy rind. It is ripened for two weeks. It has a 72 per cent fat content, and is voluptuously rich, soft and creamy.
(See *Double Crèmes.*)

SVECIAOST

Country of origin: Sweden.

Background: The Swedes originally created this cheese as a version of Gouda, but it has developed a character of its own.

Description: Made from cow's milk (sometimes skimmed) Sveciaost is made in wheel shapes weighing 11 kg to 13 kg (25-30 lb). The cheese has a smooth, waxed rind with a white interior scattered with small, irregularly shaped holes. In texture the cheese is firm, elastic, supple.

Numerous types of this cheese are made throughout Sweden. Fat content can vary between 30 and 60 per cent; it can be ripened for six weeks or left to mature for as long as a year; some versions are spiced with caraway seeds or a combination of caraway seeds and cloves; some are unflavoured.

All these factors affect its taste; essentially an uncomplicated, mild, bland, buttery Gouda-like cheese when young. Aged versions gain considerably in depth of taste and strength and can be quite pungent; spiced Sveciaosts are tangy and aromatic.

Wines: Simple dry reds and whites; beer.
Serve: A good snack-type cheese.
Fat content: 30-60 per cent.
Type: Bland/buttery.
Aroma: Unpronounced.

SWEET MUENSTER

A processed cheese more commonly known as Mun-Chee. The cheese is made in loaf shapes and is soft, sweet and simple—it has nothing in common with the notable French cheese, Münster.

SWEDISH FONTINA

A copy of the famous Italian cheese—rather more full flavoured than the original.
(See *Fontina.*)

TAFFEL

Country of origin: Denmark.

Background: The word *taffel* means 'table'; the cheese is a member of the Danish family of Samsoe table cheeses. The Danes now call the cheese Tybo but versions of Taffel cheese are made in several other countries.

Description: The cheese can be made in rectangular or loaf shapes in weights varying from 1.5-2.5 kg (3-6 lb). A standard size measures 19 cm by 12 cm by 12 cm (8 x 5 x 5 in). Taffel has a dry and yellowish rind often covered with a red or yellow wax. Its interior is pure yellow to white, smooth and close in texture with a few small holes and a supple, resilient body. The flavour is mild, bland and buttery.

Wines: Light whites and reds.
Serve: A good all-purpose table cheese whose slicing qualities make it ideal for sandwiches and snacks; it goes well with fruit and its mildness makes it appealing to children.
Fat content: 40-45 per cent.
Type: Bland/buttery.
Aroma: Unpronounced.

TALEGGIO

Country of origin: Italy.

Background: Taleggio is a stracchino style cheese of the *dolce* (mild) category which can be compared to Bel Paese. It comes from the Taleggio Valley in Lombardy.

Description: The cheese is pressed, uncooked, surface-ripened, and made in the shape of a 20 cm (8 in) square block 5 cm (2 in) thick. Its outer rind is rough, uneven and rosy-pink in colour; the interior varies from creamy-white to light yellow. Taleggio is semi-soft but supple and springy-feeling to the touch. It is mild but rich in flavour, full and creamy. The cheese is made from cow's milk and is ripened for about two months, the flavour growing sharper with age.

Wines: Light but lively reds and whites.
Serve: A delicious, rich, creamy cheese to serve at the end of meals with fruit.
Fat content: 48 per cent.
Type: Bland/buttery.
Aroma: Unpronounced.
(See *Stracchino*.)

TELEMES

Country of origin: Greece.

Background: This cheese is produced in several Balkan countries and is similar to Feta.

Description: Telemes is made from sheep's milk (and sometimes goat's milk) in 7.5 to 10 cm (3-4 in) squares about 5 cm (2 in) thick. The cheese is soft, moist, and creamy white in colour, and is ripened for ten days in a salt bath. Like Feta it is often called a 'pickled' cheese and is very sharp and salty to the taste.

Wines: Retsina, ouzo.
Serve: Suited for savouries, hors d'oeuvres and on cheese platters complementing dark rye breads and stuffed olives; can also be used lightly crumbled into salads.
Fat content: 40 per cent.
Type: Sheep's milk/pickled.
Aroma: Unpronounced but has a salty note.

TETE DE MOINE

This cheese is also known as Bellelaye. It is a Swiss cheese which dates back to the fifteenth century. At the monastery of Bellelaye, where the cheese originated, it was the practice for each monk to receive one cheese (per head)— hence its name. Tête de Moine resembles a more strongly flavoured Gruyère.
(See *Bellelaye*.)

TEXAS LONGHORN

(See American *Cheddars*.)

THURGAUER

A Swiss cheese similar to Royalp but with a richer, sweeter flavour.
(See *Royalp*.)

TIGER

Brand name for a Swiss range of processed cheese.
(See *Processed Cheese*.)

TILLAMOOK

An American Cheddar from Oregon—tangy and full flavoured.
(See American *Cheddars*.)

TILSIT

Country of origin: Germany.

Background: This cheese was first produced by Dutch settlers in the region of Tilsit, East Prussia, in the middle of last century. It is also known as Ragnit and is made in several other countries apart from Germany.

Description: Tilsit is made in small wheel shapes or rectangular loaves. The round variety usually measures 25 cm (10 in) in diameter and 12.5 cm (5 in) thick. In colour the cheese varies from ivory to pale yellow, with a slightly darker rind (there is also a rindless variety).

The Germans place Tilsit in their sliceable (schnittkäse) cheese category. It has a supple, resilient texture and contains numerous small holes the size of barley grains.

With their love of strong tasting cheese, the Germans sometimes make pungent, full-bodied versions of Tilsit, but often the cheese is tangy, piquant and mildly sour, somewhere between a mild Limburger and a strong Port Salut.

Tilsit is made from cow's milk, a surface-ripened cheese which is cured for between four and six months. One variety made from skim milk is flavoured with caraway seeds to give it a spicier, sharper, more pronounced flavour.

The cheese is wrapped in tinfoil or parchment before marketing.

Norwegian Tilsit is medium to sharp tasting with a rather strong aroma and a drier texture.

Wines: Liebfraumilch and spätlese style whites; reds; tawny port.
Serve: End of meals; its easy slicing qualities make it suitable for sandwiches.
Fat content: 45 per cent.
Type: Monastery.
Aroma: Varies, with age—can be noticeably pungent.

TOMMES

The word tomme simply means 'cheese' and prefixes the names of many cheeses produced in the Savoy Mountains of France.

The best known of the tommes is Tomme de Savoie, a cheese made in a cylindrical shape of 20 cm (8 in) diameter and up to 12.5 cm (5 in) thick. The cheese has a natural greyish rind dotted with reddish pigmentation and a supple-textured yellow-white interior. In taste the cheese is mildly tangy with the attractive earthy quality found in many monastery-style cheeses. The cheese is ripened for two months and is made from cow's milk. When made from goat's milk it is known as Tomme de Chèvres.

Tomme au Marc is an unusual and striking-looking variety which is partly ripened in, and covered with, a mixture of grape pulp, skins and pips. This cheese has a sharp, pronounced taste and a full, alcoholic aroma.

Other cheeses of the tommes family include Tomme au Fenouil, Tomme du Revard and Tomme Boudane. The majority of these cheeses are unlikely to be seen outside France.

TOMMES DES NEIGES

This cheese, which comes from the French Alps, is one of numerous mountain cheeses known as 'tommes' or sometimes 'tomes' (this is simply a dialect word for 'cheese'). This particular tomme derives the second part of its name from its rind which is snow white. The interior is ivory colour, semi-soft and dotted with tiny eyes. Although not overstrong in flavour, the cheese has a distinctive tang and attractive earthy quality.
(See *Tommes*.)

TOMMES DES PYRENEES

A French mountain cheese similar in texture and taste to Doux de Montagne, both related

Selection of Danish cheeses, members of the Samsoe family (from top, left to right) Samsoe, Tybo, Maribo, Molbo, Fynbo, Mini Fynbo, Baby Fynbo (photo by Russell Cockayne)

to Chilberta. Tommes des Pyrenees is milder—
a semi-soft cheese with a black wax rind.
(See *Chilberta*.)

TOMME DU POITOU

A cheese from the Poitou region of France
made from an equal mixture of goat's and
cow's milk. The cheese is about 20 cm (8 in) in
diameter and has a white downy rind. A semi-
soft cheese, not as sharp as regular goat's milk
cheeses.
(See *Chèvres*.)

TRAPPIST

Trappist is a general term for a monastery style
cheese originated by Trappist monks. According to some authorities it is also the name of a
cheese first produced in Bosnia in 1885. Cheese
of this style is now made in several European
countries including Hungary, Czechoslovakia
and Germany.

All these cheeses are similar in style to Port
Salut and Saint Paulin. The Canadian version
is Oka.
(See *Port Salut*, *Saint Paulin* and *Oka*.)

TRECCIA

Background: Treccia is similar to Mozzarella,
but is made in a plaited shape. It belongs to the
pasta filata or drawn curd family of Italian
cheeses.

Description: Treccia is a soft, moist white
cheese with a plastic body and a smooth, close
texture. Made in a plaited shape, the cheese
weighs between 250 g and 500 g ($\frac{1}{2}$-1 lb) and
undergoes a ripening period of only two to
three days. The cheese has little aroma and a
mild creamy flavour, rather delicate. It is made
from cow's milk.

Wines: Light whites and reds.
Serve: Chiefly used in cooking: when heated
the cheese forms long elastic strands, making
it ideal for pizzas.

Fat content: 40-45 per cent.
Type: Fresh, unripened.
Aroma: Unpronounced.

TRIPLE CREMES

Country of origin: France.

Background: This type of cheese, now produced all over Europe, is a step up from the
double crème type. The French define a triple
crème as one which contains 75 per cent
matière grasse, which means that butterfat
accounts for 75 grams out of every 100 grams
of cheese. Such information is always detailed
on the cheese's packaging. Most cheeses have
an average 45 per cent fat content. Consequently, triple crèmes are the richest and the
creamiest of cheeses. They are also relative
newcomers, having first appeared in the 1950s.

Description: Triple crèmes are usually made in
small cylinder shapes about 7.5 cm (3 in) in
diameter and 5 cm (2 in) thick. Other shapes
include squares and wheels. These cheeses are
made from cow's milk enriched with cream,
and are usually ripened for about three weeks,
when they develop a light bloomy mould on
their surfaces, sometimes pigmented. They are
usually creamy white in colour. Some varieties
such as Fontainebleau are unripened.

As mentioned earlier, in taste and texture
triple crèmes are the richest, softest and
creamiest cheeses of all, sometimes having a
sourish piquant tinge—uncomplicated but
voluptuous and delicious.

Triple crèmes are sold under different brand
names such as Bellétoile, Boursault, Brillat-
Savarin, Lucullus, Explorateur, Magnum and
Saint André.

Wines: Light spätlese-style whites; rosés; they
also go with coffee.
Serve: A good choice instead of a dessert at the
end of a meal; as a luxurious and totally self-
indulgent snack with wafers of crisp apple or
pear, or simply with cracker biscuits.
Fat content: 75 per cent.
Type: Triple crème.
Aroma: Unpronounced.

Bellétoile (left), a Triple Crème Cheese, and Rondelé, a Double Crème

TROPEFYNBO

A version of the Danish cheese Fynbo made with a thicker rind designed to enable it to withstand high temperatures.
(See *Fynbo*.)

TWIN FLATS

(See American *Cheddars*.)

TYBO

Country of origin: Denmark.

Background: Another member of the Danish family of Samsoe cheeses. It was once called Taffel.

Description: Tybo is a rectangular, loaf-shaped cheese measuring 19 cm by 12 cm by 12 cm (8 x 5 x 5 in) It has a dry, yellowish rind which may be covered with red or yellow wax. Its texture is firm and supple with a limited number of regularly shaped, pea-sized holes. Its colour is pure yellow to white and like all members of the Samsoe family it is eminently suitable for slicing. Tybo is a mild-tasting cheese, bland and buttery in consistency.

Wines: Light reds or whites; beer.
Serve: An all-purpose table cheese; its mildness makes it suitable for children.
Fat content: 45 per cent.
Type: Bland/buttery.
Aroma: Unpronounced.

UNITY BLUE

Country of origin: Australia.

Background: This Queensland cheese is the only remaining blue vein variety in Australia. Production of Unity Blue began in 1960, and is still a thriving concern. It is made at Too-woomba, Queensland.

Description: Unity Blue has a pale creamy body with a fairly open cracked texture and a generous veining of blue-green mould creating its rich piquant flavour. It is distributed throughout the eastern states of Australia in 2 kg (4½ lb) wheels and 125 g (¼ lb) foil wrapped wedges. The cheese is aged for approximately four months. To the taste it is quite sharp and tangy.

Wines: Fruity reds.
Serve: Unity Blue is complemented by dried apricots, muskatels or crisp salad vegetables. It can be easily crumbled into quiches, hot breads, salad or vegetable dressings and savoury butters.
Fat content: 48-50 per cent.
Type: Blue vein.
Aroma: Mould smell.

VACCHINO ROMANO

This Italian cheese is related to Pecorino Romano but instead of being made from sheep's milk, it is made from cow's milk. Primarily used as a hard, grating cheese.
(See *Pecorino Romano*.)

VACHERIN FRIBOURGEOIS

Country of origin: Switzerland.

Background: This is a mountain cheese of ancient origins. It is thought most likely that it is a predecessor of Gruyère and Emmentaler developed before the cheesemakers had perfected the art of 'cooking' the cheese curd.

Description: The cheese is made in the shape of a small wheel 40 cm (16 in) in diameter and 7.5 cm (3 in) thick. Vacherin Fribourgeois is made from cow's milk and has a thin, washed and brushed rind which can vary in colour from yellowish to pinkish. It is a pleasant tasting cheese which can be considered a milder, whiter type of Gruyère, lacking that cheese's complexity but palatable and faintly aromatic.

It should be noted that there are several other Vacherin cheeses made both in Switzerland and in the Savoy mountain area of

France. These include Vacherin d'Abondance, Vacherin des Aillons and Vacherin des Beauges. Vacherin Mont d'Or, a variety widely seen overseas, has a moist, pinkish rind and an interior paste so soft it is almost liquid. These cheeses are often so runny they can be eaten with a spoon.

Wines: Any light and fruity wine.
Serve: End of meals; also used in fondues.
Fat content: 45 per cent.
Type: Monastery.
Aroma: Unpronounced.

VACHERIN MONT D'OR

A Swiss mountain cheese that is made in flat cylinder shapes about 30 cm (12 in) thick. The cheese has a thin, pinkish rind and an interior so soft as to be almost liquid. Such cheeses are often so runny they can be eaten with a spoon. A mild flavoured cheese, faintly aromatic and creamy. To fully enjoy a runny Vacherin, the cheese should not be sliced. The rind should be removed and then the cheese eaten with a spoon. The French make a version of this cheese bearing the same name. These cheeses are members of the Vacherin cheese family produced in mountain areas by both the French and the Swiss.
(See *Vacherin Fribourgeois*.)

VALAIS RACLETTE

A Swiss cheese whose name is synonymous with a special toasted dish. The cheese is more commonly known as Raclette.
(See *Raclette*.)

VALEMBERT

A part skimmed cow's milk cheese made in Camembert style with a white bloomy rind. The cheese does not run as Camembert does when cut, it is not as rich and creamy, but it has a mild Camembert flavour to it—not as exciting as the true Camembert but a cheese that gives the feeling of this style of cheese while having the bonus of a low fat content. (See *Camembert*.)

VALENCAY

Country of origin: France.

Background: A goat's milk cheese from the Berry region of France, made in the shape of a small pyramid with the top cut off. Because of its shape it is sometimes known as Pyramide.

Description: Valençay is a soft, bloomy rind cheese about 7.5 cm (3 in) high and 7.5 cm by 7.5 cm (3 x 3 in) at its base. The cheese is cured for up to one month when it develops a fine downy white rind. Some varieties are coated with wood ash, which gives a bluish colour to the rind.
Valençay is quite mild-tasting with a lightly 'goatish' aroma and flavour to it; aged cheeses are considerably more pungent.
Other goat's milk cheeses made in a similar pyramid shape are Levroux and Pouligny Saint Pierre.

Wines: Fruity red and white wines.
Serve: End of meals to add balance to a cheese board.
Fat content: 45 per cent.
Type: Goat's milk.
Aroma: Noticeable but not over-pronounced.

VENETO

One of the lesser known of the Italian Grana style cheeses. These are cheeses that can be matured for two to three year periods. They develop very hard, brittle textures and are predominantly used in cooking as grating cheeses. The most famous is Parmesan.
(See *Grana* and *Parmesan*).

VENEZZA

An Italian grating cheese belonging to the Grana family of cheeses, the most famous of which is Parmesan.
(See *Grana* and *Parmesan*.)

VERMONT

A highly rated American Cheddar; a variety is Vermont Sage, spiced with sage flavouring. (See American *Cheddars*.)

VIEUX PANE

A large sized Pont l'Evêque which is made in a 35 cm (14 in) square, 2.5 cm (1 in) thick. Because of its size it does not dry out as quickly as the smaller Pont l'Evêque—a good point to remember when you're dealing with an imported cheese as temperamental as Pont l'Evêque. While it is rated as one of the top four French cheeses it is difficult to get in the peak of its condition outside France. Too often it dries out and develops a bitter, mouldy taste. (See *Pont l'Evêque*.)

WARSAWSKI

A Polish sheep's milk cheese similar to Kashkaval and Kasseri. An American version of Warsawski is made which is less strong and more 'Cheddary' in taste than the original Polish cheese.
(See *Kashkaval* and *Kasseri*.)

WEISSLACKER

Country of origin: Germany.

Background: This very spicy and potent little cheese is a speciality of Bavaria and is typical of the strong-smelling, sharp-tasting range of traditional German cheeses. It can be compared to Limburger.

Description: This cheese is made from a combination of skimmed and whole cow's milk and usually comes in 10 cm to 12.5 cm (4-5 in) squares about 8.75 cm (3½ in) thick. The cheese looks like a white cube of paste with virtually no rind, very few holes and a smeary, glistening surface.

Weisslacker is salted and matured for a total period of seven months, in an atmosphere of high humidity. This results in a cheese with quite some punch in taste and odour—it is something of an acquired taste, being very pungent and sharply pronounced in flavour and smell.

It is sometimes known as Bierkäse.

Wine: Does not go with wine but the Germans eat them with relish with beer; sometimes *in* their beer.
Serve: As a snack with beer.
Fat content: 40 per cent.
Type: Strong smelling.
Aroma: Pronounced.

WENSLEYDALE

Country of origin: Great Britain (England).

Background: Another very old English cheese from the Ure Valley area in Yorkshire. Its recipe is said to have been brought to England by Cistercian monks who came after the Norman Conquest in 1066. The recipe fell into the hands of local farmers' wives when the monks fled after Henry VIII ravaged Jervaulx Abbey in the sixteenth century.

Description: There are two types of Wensleydale—a white and a blue. The white takes only three weeks to mature, is clean, mild and just slightly salty to the taste, is attractively crumbly and noted for its delicious honeyed aftertaste. This last point accounts for White Wensleydale going extremely well with apple pie—a favourite combination in the north of England.

Blue Wensleydale is hard to come by nowadays, although it used to be plentiful before World War II. It is a richer, more full-bodied cheese than the white, like most good blues taking six months to mature. Rich, creamy, both tangy and sweet, it is considered by cheese buffs to be a rival to Stilton.

Wines: White Wensleydale with a light burgundy; serve the Blue with a light port or rosé.
Serve: Try the White with apple pie as a dessert; end of meals for the Blue.

Wensleydale (top and centre), Caerphilly (below)

Fat content: 45 per cent.
Type: Cheddar family/blue vein.
Aroma: The White, unpronounced; Blue Wensleydale has a tangy aroma.

WHITE GORGONZOLA

A stracchino cheese—a Gorgonzola which does not take on the greenish-blue veining of the famous Italian cheese. It is also known as Pannerone.
(See *Pannerone* and *Stracchino*.)

WHITE STILTON

A Stilton cheese which does not develop the network of veining that would make the cheese a blue vein.
(See *Stilton*.)

WILSTERMARSCH

Country of origin: Germany.

Background: The Germans place this cheese in a semi-soft category of sliceable cheeses that includes Steinbüscher, Edelpilz, Butter Cheese and Weisslacker. Wilstermarsch comes from the Schleswig-Holstein region near the Danish border. It can be considered a variety of Tilsit.

Description: The cheese, made from cow's milk, is usually produced in the shape of a loaf for ease of slicing. It has a supple texture, is dotted with small holes and is a rich shiny yellow in colour. During its ripening period large quantities of salt are added, which gives the cheese's surface a yellowish-white, lacquer-like coating. In taste, not overpowering, but sharpish, slightly sour.

Wines: Light whites and reds.
Serve: End of meals, snacks; the Germans recommend the cheese with sausage, ham and mushrooms.
Fat content: 45 per cent.
Type: Monastery.
Aroma: Unpronounced.

WINDSOR RED

Country of origin: Great Britain (England).

Background: In recent years several English companies have taken to making variations of traditional English cheeses. This is one—a blend of Cheddar with red wine.

Description: Windsor Red is an attractive-looking cheese, pale yellow in colour, mottled with red veining throughout; it looks good on a cheese board. The cheese is aged up to five months and has the characteristic clean, creamy Cheddar taste with a light flavour of red wine. Windsor Red is a close textured cheese, firm and slightly crumbly.

Wines: Light reds; beer.
Serve: End of meals; snacks.
Fat content: 45 per cent.
Type: Cheddar family.
Aroma: Unpronounced.

WORIENER

Another German cheese that is related to Limburger. The cheese is made in small 10 cm (4 in) square shapes.
(See *Limburger*.)

YOUNG AMERICAN

(See American *Cheddars*.)

ZIGER

A whey, Cottage style cheese, the best known version of which is Ricotta.
(See *Ricotta*.)

ZOMMA

A Turkish sheep's milk cheese similar to the better known Balkan cheese Kashkaval.
(See *Kashkaval*.)

Windsor Red (top), Derby Sage (below)